ABUNDANT
PATHS

**Beyond Either/Or Thinking to Fulfilling
LGBTQIA Relationships That Last**

ABUNDANT
PATHS

**Beyond Either/Or Thinking to Fulfilling
LGBTQIA Relationships That Last**

Karl W. Beckstrand, M.A.

The author wishes to extend special thanks to Chris, A.J, Adrianne, Anna, Brian, Michele, Robert, Scott, Susan, and Heather.

C. S. Lewis extracts reprinted by permission, ©C.S. Lewis Pte. Ltd. 1960.

Published by Paths Press (an imprint of Premio Publishing)
Midvale, UT, USA. Order direct, or via any major distributor
PremioPublishing.com

Library of Congress Catalog Number: 2022947036
ISBN: 978-1951599188

For David

Table of Contents

Trailhead

CLOSE BEYOND IMAGINATION

MORE THAN A THIRD OF AMERICANS say they are chronically lonely.[1] Achieving lasting, happy relationships is a challenge for just about anyone; for LGBTQIA people, it can seem impossible.

Our greatest joys come via relationships. For decades, I dreamed of deep, lasting human connection, only to experience repeated disappointment. Somewhere in my twenties, I concluded that the kind of bonding I desired might not be possible. But life has a way of surprising us. Today, I feel my relationships are more profound, stable, and rewarding than I had dreamed, and perhaps more than most people do. Turns out, I only had to let go of the poor ways of relating and leave behind the unhelpful ideas that I'd clung to. I'd like to share with you how you might have this contentment as well.

People often see only binary options, including in relationships (perhaps especially in LGBTQIA relating: you're either "out" or in the closet). Simplistic views reduce our available options and minimize our chances for deep connection.

Yet, there are infinite ways to be human, to relate as humans, let alone as LGBTQIA individuals. There may be better ways to love and be loved, regardless of orientation, than the standard ways the world often signals.[2] I'm convinced that *all* men—heterosexual *and* gay—have the capacity to love each other intensely and lastingly. I believe women enjoy this same gift (regardless of sexual orientation). Activities segregated by sex in history were not always driven by mores; men often prefer the company of men, and women often prefer to associate with other women.

I'm not typically someone who publishes intimate details of my life, but I feel that what I've learned is too important not to share. Most of my words are directed to people with same-sex attraction—this term is used here, instead of "gay," to include people, like me, who are also attracted to the opposite sex (*bisexual, biromantic,* or *bi*). My experience is individual and comes from a "male" perspective, and some of what I say may not apply to all same-sex–attracted people. While I address families and friends of LGBTQIA people in the epilogue, I hope anyone will gain perspective from this entire discussion.

Is someone you love struggling with LGBTQIA matters or relationships? Are you? This book offers unique insights, positive views on differences and how they can enrich individuals and society as a whole.[3]

I've found that people can easily read their own story as they peruse mine. If what you read here seems very much like your story, consider that, besides learning from the experiences we share, you can benefit from what is unique about my story.

If you're usually a fast reader or you like to leapfrog through chapters, I'd invite you to slow your usual pace for this book. Sitting a while with concepts can prevent misunderstanding, and sometimes the mind needs time to mull over new ideas. It's okay if you don't agree with me, though I hope you'll keep these thoughts in mind for future insight. Keeping one's options open allows the greatest possibility for fulfilment.[4]

Is this a "change" book? Yes—but not in the way you might think. This book deals with changes that all people could benefit from (and the change isn't in sexual orientation). Rather than reduce opportunities for love, I wish to deepen and extend love's unique expressions to a variety of spheres.

The discussion of human interpersonal relationships, including sexuality, is constantly expanding and shifting. Terminology changes. In the space of my own life, I've seen many terms emerge and fall out of fashion. There are terms that I still use out of habit or because they're comfortable for me. To provide clarity as I tell my story, I've provided definitions here of terms I use frequently. The appendixes offer more information.

DEFINITIONS

- For the purposes of this book, *having sex* and *being sexual* refer broadly to ways of interacting with people that typically lead to sexual climax.
- *Sex* (biological) and *gender* (societal/cultural) are technically not synonyms, but I use them interchangeably in this book (except when *sex* refers to coitus or sexual stimulation) because that's generally how they're used by laypeople.
- The *Q* in LGBTQIA can stand for "queer" (which is sometimes used broadly here, like gay, to refer to any LGBTQIA person), but it can also stand for "questioning" (see Appendix B).
- *I* in LGBTQIA stands for "intersex" (previously known as *hermaphrodite*).
- *A* at the end of LGBTQIA represents "asexual." Asexuals use *ace* for short.

One important aspect of learning to think about things in new ways is learning how to talk about ideas differently. Learning and using new terminology, or repurposing old terms, might feel awkward or even uncomfortable at first. But using respectful and appropriate terminology is one way of showing love and respect for all and for the differences in our journeys. I'm still learning this, but more precise use of language helps us break out of confining, binary ways of thinking that prevent us from finding the love and happiness we are meant to enjoy. [5]

> *"The goal is not to change who you are*
> *but to become more of who you are at your best." [6]*
>
> —Sally Hogshead

NOTES

1. Richard Weissbourd et al., "Loneliness in America: How the Pandemic Has Deepened an Epidemic of Loneliness and What We Can Do about It," Making Caring Common Project, Harvard Graduate School of Education, last modified February 2021, https://mcc.gse.harvard.edu/reports/loneliness-in-america. Prior to COVID-19, a Cigna survey said 3 of 5 people are lonely. Elena Renken, "Most Americans Are Lonely, And Our Workplace Culture May Not Be Helping," National Public Radio, January 23, 2020, https://www.npr.org/sections/health-shots/2020/01/23/798676465/most-americans-are-lonely-and-our-workplace-culture-may-not-be-helping. See also "Why Men Are Lonelier in America Than Elsewhere," *The Economist*, January 1, 2022, https://www.economist.com/united-states/2022/01/01/why-men-are-lonelier-in-america-than-elsewhere; "Donate: Help the Foundation for Male Studies Meet Its Objective," Foundation for Male Studies, https://www.malestudies.org/donate.

2. Most of us delicately try to hold both truth and love (I doubt any of us do it perfectly)—one virtue without the other

can be a vice. I did write a book, the subtitle of which is *Communication Guaranteed Not to Offend.* This is not that book—and *that* book was a gag, since such communication seems to elude us mortals.

3. The King James Bible (London, 1769/2017), Isa. 55:8; 1 Sam. 16:7.

4. Some people tell me they have explored the kind of connectedness I discuss in this book without seeing a payoff. When I probe, they acknowledge that they tried to combine two inadequate ways of relating (or never truly let go of old ways of relating). To truly experience profound and resilient connection, some things are best let go or avoided.

5. See https://PremioBooks.com for expanded notes and active links (see QR code at the end of the book).

6. Sally Hogshead, Quotss.com, SoftCopy IT Services Pvt. Ltd., accessed August 17, 2022, http://www.quotss.com/quote/The-goal-is-not-to-change-who-you-are-but-to-become-more-of-who-you-are-at.

7. As not everyone is comfortable with the world knowing their personal situation or status, I have changed nearly all friends' names in this book, and I sometimes use the vague reference "personal social media post" (with the "names" and permission of the authors) where applicable.

CHAPTER 1
Out of Bounds

Why would you stay in an organization that doesn't want you?
You're a repressed sheep—blindly following what a flawed preacher
tells you to do. You should quit your church and live the way you want
to live.

PEOPLE SAY THINGS LIKE THIS WHEN they learn I'm an active churchgoer—and that I, a man, am attracted to both men and women.[1] I tend to smile and laugh it off, but few wounds go deeper than being misunderstood.

When people make these statements to me, they make assumptions about me and my relationship with my faith. What many people don't know is that my history *doesn't* reflect a habit of obedience to faith leaders, personal excitement for gay sex, or feeling rejected by my church because of my sexual orientation. Clearly, attraction to one's own sex doesn't mean the same path for everyone!

I have always wanted my own family and came close to marrying multiple times. In 2008, I ended an engagement to a woman with whom I wasn't compatible (she knew I was bi, but we had significant differences in other areas). It had been many years since I'd been sexual with a man, but because I had been sexually compulsive—out of control—for much of my early life, fear of falling back into that chaotic, destructive path caused me to become a recluse (not a great decision, but it was all I could think of at the time). It's tragic when two-option choices are all one can imagine!

I still had the friends I'd grown up with, but most were married and busy with growing families. Soon, a rift in my own family left me even more isolated.

While I know that sex can be fulfilling and lovely in ideal circumstances, I sensed that sex wasn't what I lacked. Based on my experiences, I felt sure that sex (in my case) would take me farther away from what I needed, but I had no idea how to find true connection.

This book is not about addiction—though sex addiction has given me key insights on broader topics. My experience informs me; you and your experience may not harmonize with mine, but I believe that the things I've learned can be applied to a variety of experiences and circumstances to help people find fulfillment in all their same-sex relationships.

Today, I am no longer disconnected, but I'm not compulsive in my behavior, either. I love who I am—feelings and all! I don't experience shame regarding my orientation; I'm grateful I'm attracted to men. I have incredibly deep long-term relationships, and I have peace about who I am and my worth. But there is a lot more detail on how I came to appreciate *all* of my feelings.

POINTS TO PONDER

- Is Sexual Orientation a Choice? Sexual *orientation* is not a defect, it's not a sin, it's not contagious, it's not a mortal choice, and it's not an act of rebellion. People choose their actions, but feelings are not in our hands quite the same way. We can exert influence over feelings, but often, we simply feel what we feel. Note that sexual orientation is a set of feelings and impulses, while sex is a set of actions. We can learn to manage our feelings, but we do not choose the feelings themselves. Consider this: Why would anyone *choose* to be mostly attracted to a group where most of its members (men, in my case) would *not* reciprocate and might even react negatively to such attraction?

- Our greatest joys come via relationships, yet long-term relationship bliss is elusive, regardless of sexual orientation.

- I believe there is purpose in our differences. What might those purposes be? What about differences in our sexualities?

- Few choices are binary, and either/or options are often artificial when it comes to human relationships. There are infinite ways to be human, let alone LGBTQIA. There may be better ways to love and be loved (regardless of orientation) than the standard ways the world signals. In what ways can thinking beyond the binary open us to other options?

NOTES

1. The following is written by Blake Fisher, inclusion advisor at Brigham Young University:

   I'm curious if celibate, Buddhist monks [ever hear] the following:

   - It's so sad that your [tradition] "forces" you to give up sex and "makes" you live this way.

   - A loving God would never ask you to sacrifice anything that feels good or could make you happy.

   - Your life is going to be so sad and meaningless without a romantic, sexual relationship.

   - I can't believe your church tells you what to eat, what to wear, and how to live . . . so controlling.

   - Do you wonder if you're living this way because of fear . . . fear of rejection, of your own desires, of hell, the unknown?

   - I once knew someone who was a celibate monk, they were so much happier after they left, you should leave too.

   - Don't worry, your church is eventually going to change (catch up with the times) . . . and then you'll be happy.

   - Even if you've found peace and joy on your journey, it's probably best that you keep it to yourself so others don't feel pressured to live the same way. (Personal social media post, 2022)

CHAPTER 2
Either/Or?

Who are you?

SO, YOU'RE GAY OR BISEXUAL OR otherwise queer. What does that look like for you? What does it mean? Perhaps you assumed or were told by someone that you must avoid contact with those of your sex. If you've (rightly) concluded that you can't do that—that you somehow need those of your sex—what will your relationships look like? Will they be close? Exclusive? Lasting? I have ample evidence that you *do* need those of your sex and that you and the things that make you unique are *needed* in society (perhaps especially among those of your own sex).

Why talk about this? Author Meghan Decker says people can feel isolated by differences—hopeless. Some can't heal or even receive love, much less give love, until they feel that their core self is known and accepted. I have experienced this. Many people are still trying to figure out who they really are at their core. Until this happens, a counterproductive "us versus them" worldview can be difficult to shake. Whether you only need to "come out of the closet" to be honest with yourself or with others, know that coming out removes barriers, but it doesn't create wholeness on its own; there are wondrous options beyond this!

You are not in a separate class based on your feelings or your behavior—neither are you inferior to heterosexual people. They experience frustration, heartbreak, and pain as well; not everything always goes their way.[3] Decker explains that while isolation, shame, and hopelessness aren't inherent in being LGBTQIA, these feelings are often attached to these orientations:

> Why do I need to come out when I don't plan to leave . . . my [mixed orientation] marriage—when I'm not changing anything? Because being honest and open does change everything. It relieves me of the shame that has shadowed my life for decades. This is especially important for [people] who may have internalized judgment, rejection, and shame. The incongruence between how we are seen and the inner reality of our lives is excruciating. We might feel we are deceiving those around us, both family and friends. We are afraid of the rejection we *might* feel if others saw us as we really are. Our perception of ourselves becomes dark and distorted. . . .
>
> After I came out publicly to my friends and family, I felt as though I could breathe deeply for the first time in my adult life. I didn't realize how tightly I held myself, and fear of discovery limited every relationship. I was friendly but fearful, caring yet careful. My family and friends have so much more of me now because I'm not hiding.[1]

The insights I'll be sharing with you have been hard-won through my experiences; through struggles with my beliefs, sexuality, addiction, and relationships; and, ultimately, through peace and fulfillment via deep connections. For background, I'll share with you some things about where I'm coming from.

I grew up in San Jose, California. I love that one-time agricultural area that morphed into Silicon Valley before my eyes.

I was raised by a liberal mom and a conservative dad. I won't detail the mutual rejection between my father and me; some people explain away homosexuality as being the result of a poor relationship with a same-sex parent, but I believe the explanations for same-sex attraction are multiple and complex, and I don't pretend to have a grasp on them. A lot of people attracted to their own sex had close, affectionate relationships with their same-sex parent. I did not.[2]

My mother had severe health challenges. My father resented having had a family, as his first love (he'd probably concede) was his motorcycle and the open road. His time and resources went to that love. My older siblings remember parents who loved each other. I remember warfare.

As the youngest of four kids, I was loved but neglected. My mom's health prevented her from seeing that we left the house "kempt." My dad's spending meant we occasionally went without food, clothing, or heat. The result was that I didn't always appear well cared for, and this invited rejection and abuse from peers (I was also not nimble or street smart).

When I was about 12 years old I poured my heart out to my dad in a letter, asking him to love me. He never acknowledged I'd even written him. Having said this, I cannot ignore the advantages I had growing up with a father present who usually provided for me and offered an example of work, sport, and creativity.

Like many boys, from an early age I noticed men with keen interest—though I didn't have sexual thoughts about them until sex was shown to me.

I was pulled into sexual activity by a male peer when I was eight years old.[3] I didn't want sexual interest in men, and I agonized about not being "normal." No one had instructed me on sex or on how to avoid premature sexual relating—certainly not with guys. Over the next decade, before my church mission, I was sexually active on and off. Looking back at my eight- to nineteen-year-old self, I admire my determination and (often futile) efforts to avoid sex, though it had been, I feel, thrust on me.

My parents separated when I was in the seventh grade. This was a great hardship, though my dad tried to bolster us while my mom was away. They got back together when I was in high school, but the battle raged on, and I was in no mood to be parented after having to fend for myself for most of my childhood.

While I have always been attracted to women, I didn't experience physical attraction for them until I was in my mid-to-late teens. People who have never experienced attraction to both sexes have a hard time believing that bisexuals/biromantics exist. We do! People who've never experienced *no* desire for sex have a hard time believing that asexual people exist, but they absolutely do.[4]

I am *not* asexual. As someone who is mostly attracted to my own sex, I lived much of my life believing I had two choices:

1. Engage in gay sex and perhaps settle down with a gay partner
2. Marry someone of the opposite sex and try to find happiness in "straight" life

Both of these options left me wanting for something that I intuited was important to my happiness. Only later would I grasp that *most* choices involve far more than two options![5]

You may or may not believe in a higher power; I do. In this book, I won't comment on whether God/the universe made me bi or whether he makes people gay; I don't know. I think that God is *never* surprised by anything we experience (and that there's benefit in any experience—blissful or painful). I hope you'll see examples of this in my story and perhaps see similar patterns in your own life.[6]

While I had some nurturing men in my life, they were so rare they felt almost nonexistent. Based on how I was treated by peers, I didn't consider myself attractive. Aside from sexual partners, I was mostly a loner as a child.

One thing I consistently desired but didn't get much of (other than from my mom) was physical touch and affection. Our culture already minimizes and even discourages touch, especially among males, but societal aversion to homosexuality and recent health scares have exacerbated people's fears; we generally don't share enough physical touch.

When I was growing up, men with the greatest same-sex emotional needs could typically only find connection with gay men, and in my experience, there was usually a price for affection. The expectation is generally if you want touch and connection, you must be willing for the encounter to become sexual. I recall being a young man about to get sexual with a man, but wishing only to be held. True, I *was* a youth bursting with hormones, but the pity was that I was unaware of men who might connect with me in non-sexual ways. Though I often wanted simple affection, I felt obligated to be sexual; it seemed the only path to connect with a man. Otherwise, my life seemed to consist mostly of rejection.

Ugh—I'm evil! I'm disgusting! Repent. To say that confessing my sexual deeds to my bishop filled me with terror would be an understatement. What if my family and peers found out? That could escalate ill treatment in a big way.

I feared being cast out, shunned. I'd never heard of a minor being excommunicated, but (I speculated) that must have been because no kid had done the things that I had! So often, our fears are a baseless waste of energy. Eventually, my desire for a clean conscience won. It wasn't a one-and-done confession, but my church leaders were kind, and terror instantly transformed to relief and peace.

Finally, in high school, I found friends and skills that boosted my confidence. I wasn't a jock (I was always puny until a growth spurt my senior year, when I discovered volleyball), though I enjoyed art and had leading roles in school plays.

It's fortunate that there was no public internet when I was young, or I may have hooked up with a lot more men before my mission and perhaps would have been too enmeshed in sex to believe it possible to stop.

My church leaders were gentle and supportive of my goal to serve a mission. They assured me of my worth and expressed confidence in my abilities. I recognize that not everyone in my situation gets such love; my heart aches for any that don't.

After a period of abstinence, medical exams, and having my wisdom teeth out, I said goodbye to friends and family in California. In the Provo, Utah, Church of Jesus Christ [LDS] Missionary Training Center, a professional counselor who knew of my past challenged me to not be sexual with self or others for the entire two years of my mission (I needed to learn I could live without sex—and I needed to be a good example!). I committed—and learned a valuable secret that would help me later (once I understood it). I successfully served among the wonderful people of Chile while keeping my commitment of no sexual behavior. The key, which

I didn't know at the time, was that when we commit, our limited abilities can be augmented.

In South America I (astoundingly) learned to understand and speak Spanish and much of the Chilean vernacular. I gained an appreciation for US freedoms while living under a dictatorship. I distributed food, helped build a house, and saw lives transformed—people literally lifted out of slums. I gained lifelong friendships with some of the most generous people on earth.[7]

What I didn't realize is that a double course of antibiotics when my wisdom teeth were pulled had left my body defenseless and exposed in a microbial environment that was brand new to me. I got sick almost monthly; my body couldn't stand against the "new" invaders. The consequences of this assault would impact future options and change my life forever.

POINTS TO PONDER

- This book may have a different conclusion than you anticipate. What expectations or biases are you bringing into your reading?
- Many kids who were molested by someone of the same sex never become gay, and many who weren't molested do. What other misconceptions about the "causes" of homosexuality have you encountered?
- Bisexuals really are attracted to both sexes; asexual people really don't want sex.

- Our perception of what is negative isn't always accurate. In what ways have you benefited from experiences that weren't obviously positive?

NOTES

1. Meghan Decker, *Tender Leaves of Hope: Finding Belonging as LGBTQ Latter-day Saint Women* (Springville, UT: Cedar Fort, 2022), introduction, https://meghandecker.com/blog.
2. I nearly drowned three times as a child. My father once tried to teach me to swim without communicating that to me. As he took me into the deep end of a pool with no explanation, I panicked and fought wildly to get back into the shallow. Because of my previous experiences with water, I experienced real terror. My father experienced huge rejection: His own son didn't trust him with his safety. I imagine this cemented his defensive rejection of me that began with me pushing him away years earlier as a baby. All I anticipated from him was a volatile temperament (mostly just his raised voice). I eventually taught myself to swim when I was about ten.
3. Based on what he knew at such a young age, I later concluded that the boy who introduced me to sex had previously been molested. I make no declarations about a connection between molestation and sexual orientation here. Many kids who are molested by someone of their sex never become gay, and many who aren't molested do. (Parents: Six or seven years is not too early an age to begin to discuss sex and boundaries with your child, so long as you tailor the conversation to a child's understanding.) See Gregory M. Herek, "Facts about Homosexuality and Child Molestation," LGBPsychology.

org, n.d., https://lgbpsychology.org/html/facts_molestation. html; "Recognizing the Gift of Being Same-Sex Attracted: An Interview with SSA Women," Leading Saints, February 22, 2020, https://leadingsaints.org/recognizing-the-gift-of-be-ing-same-sex-attracted-an-interview-with-ssa-women/; Kurt Freund, Robin Watson, and Robert Dickey, "Does Sexual Abuse in Childhood Cause Pedophilia: An Exploratory Study," *Archives of Sexual Behavior* 19 (1990): 557–68, https:// pubmed.ncbi.nlm.nih.gov/2082860/; "Same-Sex Attraction is Real," My Chosen Road (blog), February 16, 2020, http:// mychosenroad.com/ssa-is-real/.

4. See "Overview," The Asexual Visibility & Education Network, n.d., https://www.asexuality.org/?q=overview.html.

5. Most choices involve *multiple* options, though we sometimes need practice seeing them. See Chip Heath and Dan Heath, *Decisive: How to Make Better Choices in Life and Work* (New York: Crown Business, 2013).

6. Bible, Gen. 50:20.

7. You may not serve a mission, but if you have the opportunity to travel—take it! It may be the best education a person can receive. I've been privileged to visit many places—and I value those experiences over all advanced degrees.

CHAPTER 3
The Beaten Path

When the subject of compulsion is discussed, inevitably there's someone who asks, "Why don't people simply exert willpower?" Aside from the obvious fault-finding of the weak-willed person, the real question is "Why is it that some people can control their appetites and others can't?"

AFTER THE HIGHS AND SUCCESSES OF my mission, I experienced the return of old struggles. Once back in the USA I had more gut discomfort, but I worked while I waited for acceptance to BYU. In Utah, I lived with my oldest brother and three or four other roommates. I was excited to be living college life, but I was white-knuckling my way through lust, naively relying on my own strength and willpower.

Willpower is deceptive; it gives the illusion that we are in control—until we realize it is insufficient. Willpower generally fails, perhaps not immediately, but always eventually; it can never be a person's ultimate strength.[1]

C. S. Lewis spoke of a kind of existence that I experienced while white-knuckling myself into the closet (thinking, erroneously, it was where God wanted me):

> If you want to make sure of keeping it intact, you must give your heart to no one. . . . Wrap it carefully round with hobbies . . . avoid all entanglements; lock it up safe in the casket or coffin of your selfishness. But in that casket—safe, dark, motionless, airless—it will change. It will not be broken; it will become unbreakable, impenetrable, irredeemable. The alternative to tragedy, or at least to the risk of tragedy, is damnation. The only place outside Heaven where you can be perfectly safe from all the dangers and perturbations of love is Hell.[2]

Staying in the closet may seem safe, but there is a trapdoor in every closet—because what we're trying to hide from is a *legitimate* need. When I was in the closet, I was all alone. I needed love, as all do (and I still need love!), but I was so determined to stay completely away from men to distance myself from temptation that I wasn't getting or giving any love at all. Closets, like C. S. Lewis's box, are dark and isolating. If we don't *step* out of closet doors, that trapdoor activates, we "fall off the wagon," and our illusion of control is lost, at least to a degree. The soul stamps and stomps until its needs are acknowledged—one way or another.[3]

PARADE OF ONE

Returning to California for the summer, I quickly and unexpectedly got sexual with a man I had just met, and I entered a spiral I could not get out of (not a great surprise considering the legitimate needs I was bottling up). By now, you're aware that I'm *not* talking about sexual needs. I had sincere emotional needs that weren't being met by "normal" socializing, but they weren't being met by my sexual relating, either.

Looking back to that time, I believe we can, in some aspects of our lives, unintentionally surrender our free will to compulsions. I was trying hard to meet my emotional needs via options that were appealing but ultimately empty. Yet, the allure was real, and so I returned again and again.

I tried to stop acting sexually; I'd mentally declare that I would never return to a certain hookup place, then would find myself there that very day. It's important to note that while I was acting compulsively with men, I was dating women, attending church, and begging God daily to help me stop seeing guys. This went on for some time. My personal religious habits—my actions of "righteousness"—couldn't save me from myself.

I remained in California and took community college classes, where I found many more sexual trysts. This wasn't simply twenty-two-year-old hormones; I could *not* stop acting out with men. I was relying on my willpower, and it clearly wasn't enough.

This was a frustrating time for me. For two full years, I had kept my promise to abstain from sexual activity, so why was it so difficult now? Why did I feel so different? I understand now that I needed this period to sort out why I was compulsive and, eventually, how to meet my needs in healthful ways.

To clarify, in discussing the social-sexual aspects of life, I'm covering three scenarios:

1. Legitimate need to connect *emotionally* with those of my sex (the average person has this to some degree).[4]

2. Physical attraction to those of my own sex (regardless of whether it's related to #1).

3. Sexual behavior that is compulsive and at a higher frequency (often with a greater number of partners) than that of the average person. This last situation may not apply to many people. I am *not* saying same-sex attraction is an addiction, only that my own behaviors around sex were compulsive.

I knew that the euphoria of sex wasn't giving me what I needed. The ironic thing is that as good as orgasm felt, sex with men never was the relationship-cementing or fulfilling thing I'd been led to believe—though I *was* trying to meet some real male need. Even while dating men I cared for, I found that sexual activities failed to connect us in a way that satisfied; rather, they left me feeling *less* connected to my partner and unfulfilled in general. Yet, I kept coming back for more, hoping baselessly (every time) for that weld.

Some might argue that the emptiness was because of my culture, but keep in mind, I didn't get church or home chastity lessons until years *after* becoming sexually active— and those lessons were *not* about avoiding sex with men. I never anticipated feeling ripped open emotionally by something that felt good physically. No adult had warned the youngster Karl that these experiences would leave me feeling hollow and low, so it's hard to attribute these empty feelings to cultural conditioning.

Guys intent on being sexual aren't easily persuaded against it. Yet, I hope that, if you find you feel as I did after engaging sexually with those of your sex, you'll remember my experiences—and especially remember what I'm going to say about meeting one's real same-sex needs.

After months of confessions, my patient bishop suggested that I do what I swore I would never do: share my deepest secrets with more people. No! I was terrified, but I went to a counselor and suggested to him that I had a split personality: I was the stereotypical "Churchy Charley," yet I was also a gay sex addict. He said I was simply one person with competing desires—and that conflicting desires are a normal part of being a human. Think of the desire-based choices you make every day; common conflicts include wanting to enjoy dessert every night versus wanting to keep trim, wanting to work to support family versus wanting to spend time with family, or wanting to complete a project versus wanting to sleep/read/watch movies/play games.

You might believe that a chunk of your life can be reduced to a struggle between your willpower and intense desires (and sometimes, those desires are contrary to your other goals); I hope to demonstrate that as we *meet* real needs healthfully, life can be rich, and overwhelming urges can become fleeting—though illuminating—notions.

For me, counseling wasn't enough. I needed peers I could identify with, people who understood my situation. The obvious obstacle was that it felt like any person who truly understood my situation wanted sex from me, and I wanted it from them—or I wanted *something* from them.

One counselor introduced me to another gay man in San Francisco who was also dissatisfied with male-on-male sex. This gay man knew one other man in the same situation, and the three of us started meeting weekly in the capital of the gay world.

At first, I felt strong sexual attraction toward these men; then, I realized that I wanted to connect with them, relate to them on an emotional level. I'd learn later about the difference between wanting sex and the important impulse toward connection.

Here, though, is where I again experienced what I had as a missionary and—for the first time—recognized it as a power outside of my own, the *only* power that ever accomplished what I could not, especially where I had previously forfeited my will to my compulsions. As I met with these men who also sought better relating, something transformational occurred.

Week after week, we three talked, hugged, and went our separate ways without being sexual. It was years before I achieved real sobriety, but these friendships marked a monumental shift for me. We three *truly* bonded; we're still in touch, decades later, and feel a special kinship. This unity is the result of a shared emotional relationship, and in my experience, its depth is not typically preserved among people of the same sex who are sexual with each other.

I had tried everything to beat compulsion—and I had always failed. By sharing my thoughts, actions, and feelings with others, I was demonstrating a sincere desire to be whole, despite obvious weakness, and chains that I had never been able to break on my own now began to burst.

This isn't uncommon for people who meet real needs and speak difficult truths.[5]

POINTS TO PONDER

- Are competing desires healthy? Like our need for food, emotional and social needs must be met and not suppressed. But sometimes our desires seem to be in competition. What can contrasting impulses teach us about our values and priorities?
- As true needs are met, seemingly overwhelming urges can become rare—though illuminating— notions, indicators that there are profound and positive reasons at the root of the desire. To what benefit might someone be attracted to their own sex?

- Willpower can manifest our determination, but it cannot be our ultimate source of strength. Have you experienced the interplay of your willpower and external forces?

- Hiding our differences and difficulties may seem an easy solution, but doing so can lead to destructive isolation. Sharing differences and struggles with others can promote growth and facilitate liberation from certain difficulties. What obstacles or fears hold you back from sharing your authentic self?

- I celebrate queerness, including same-sex attraction. Today, I no longer feel pressure to conform to my American or Christian culture. I don't care what people expect or think of me; I do what I believe is best, seeking to conform to God's will (seeking my will bogs me down). How can you celebrate your queerness, or that of a loved one, in spite of social or cultural barriers?

NOTES

1. See Colleen Harrison, *He Did Deliver Me from Bondage* (Hyrum, UT: Windhaven, 2006), https://colleencharrison. com/books/he-did-deliver-me-from-bondage/.

2. C. S. Lewis, *The Four Loves* (Boston, New York: Mariner Books, 2012), 121.

3. While a wholly inadequate bandage, addiction is a sign that a legitimate need is not being met. "[God saw] sin as springing from deep and unmet needs on the part of the sinner."

Spencer W. Kimball, "Jesus: The Perfect Leader," *Ensign*, August 1979, https://www.churchofjesuschrist.org/study/ensign/1979/08/jesus-the-perfect-leader?lang=eng.

4. "God . . . bestows two other gifts; a supernatural Need-love of Himself and a supernatural Need-love of one another." Lewis, *The Four Loves*, 129. "Heterosexual men commonly prefer the company of other men, in preference to the women with whom they may be romantically involved. This phenomenon is readily visible in the work environment, and graphically illustrated in recreational pursuits like drinking, gambling, and especially sports. Men's preference for men is based on a combination of positive identifications with [males]. . . . An almost universal fear of confrontation with inherent bisexuality dictates indirect expression of male-to-male intimacy. This is frequently in the form of activities culturally associated with masculinity and that affirm an often fragile sense of heterosexuality." Irwin Hirsch, "On Men's Preference for Men," *Gender and Psychoanalysis* 2, no. 4 (1997): 469–486, https://pep-web.org/browse/document/gap.002.0469a. See also Elwood David Watson, "Men Need Other Men in Their Lives!" The Good Men Project, October 26, 2016, https://goodmenproject.com/featured-content/men-need-men-lives-wcz/; Sarah K. McKenzie et al., "Masculinity, Social Connectedness, and Mental Health: Men's Diverse Patterns of Practice," *American Journal of Men's Health* 12, no. 5 (September 2018): 1247–61, https://doi.org/10.1177/1557988318772732.

5. God loves queer persons! (See Bible, John 3:17; 1 Cor. 15:22; Luke 4:18). I celebrate queerness; I don't believe gays are defective or that queerness is a compulsion or a choice.

Is It All About Sex?

Legitimate needs, like our need for sleep, are needs that can be met in healthful ways—but never removed.

NO MAN IS AN ISLAND

EVENTUALLY, I RETURNED TO BYU, THEN landed internships with a Massachusetts publisher and later in the US House of Representatives in Washington, DC. (This all felt miraculous, as I was an atrocious student prior to college).

After getting my undergraduate degree in journalism, I was recruited home to California to work for a technical recruiting firm; it didn't hurt that I had worked in HR for Intel and Marriott during my long summers at home. Though my family had mostly moved to Utah, I returned to the Bay Area, where I made more friends, dated many women, and sang in a rock band.

I *started* to grasp that same-sex emotional needs are legitimate to all people; for some people, they are greater than for others. Most women seem to understand this, but many men ignore it.

Earlier, I'd felt no progress, but now I was beginning to comprehend what was really happening. I can't eliminate my need for people any more than remove my need for oxygen. Human social needs must be met in healthful ways. I believe many people are detrimentally isolated because their need continues to exist whether they reach out unsuccessfully, unhealthfully, or not at all.[1]

Our US culture often raises men and women to believe that once married, women can have bosom girlfriends they share everything with, but men should be content to have their wife be their world and only occasionally go running, biking, or fishing with a buddy. Close, emotionally intimate friendships among adult men are viewed as suspect.[2]

My experience tells me that *unmet* emotional needs—which are real between men too—can easily be warped into chains. In desperation to connect with others, and often not knowing exactly what it is we lack, we look to alternatives to fill that void. Compulsive behavior can be the result.

It's not just compulsive or promiscuous sexual behavior that arises: addictions to work, online games, pornography, food, gambling, or shopping are manifestations of *real* unmet emotional or social needs. You might see yourself here, but don't beat yourself up; you've been trying to meet real needs. This book offers better ways to do that. Addiction isn't simply recreational drug use or gaming; it is the soul seeking what it lacks: relief, purpose, nourishment, and bonding with others (not necessarily via sex).[3]

The biggest way legitimate same-sex needs are turned against us is in the lie that they are *sexual* needs. We are not binary automatons with only two choices; there are more ways to connect with those of one's own sex than as a potential sexual partner or as a superficial associate—coworker, classmate, neighbor.[4] I believe both attraction and admiration play a role in *any* friendship or social connection, whether the initial draw is intellectual, emotional, physical, or in mutual interests. In my experience, the fleeting connection of sex between people of the same sex cannot hold a candle to lasting, nonsexual bonds that seem only to deepen over the years.

When we understand that the void underlying every addiction is an unmet emotional need, we're better prepared to confront our own and other's addictions and compulsions. Some well-meaning people try to counter a loved one's addiction via isolation or by withdrawing connection. Unless continued interaction with the addict is detrimental to you, can you see how this is the wrong approach? Ask instead, "What are healthful, emotionally nourishing ways to fill this chasm of need?"[5]

We all need love, affection, and healthy social connections. But is sex a need? More on that to come, but keep that question in mind during this brief discussion of attraction, promiscuity, and expectations of fidelity.

KARL W. BECKSTRAND

Most of us are familiar with the Kinsey scale used to measure sexual orientation; it has its flaws, but it's useful for a basic discussion. The Kinsey scale ranges from zero to six (x if one has no sexual attraction), zero being those physically attracted exclusively to the opposite sex (one hundred percent heterosexual) and six being those who are physically attracted exclusively to their own sex (one hundred percent homosexual). Many people are unaware of asexual people, or those who are x on the scale. Asexual people can be affectionate or not, attracted to the same or opposite sex, or somewhere in between, but they don't desire sex.[6]

Many one hundred percent "heterosexuals" or one hundred percent "homosexuals" find it difficult to believe someone could be somewhere in the middle of the scale, but a lot of us are. My attractions lean toward men, but my attraction to women puts me at about four on the scale; I have been a 3 at times, and other times a 5.

Gay men, lesbians, bisexuals, and others fall all along the spectrum. Take a simple poll of your gay friends: Ask, "How would you feel about engaging in sex with the 'opposite' sex?" I've received a variety of answers. Feelings range from revulsion to apathy to attraction. This illustrates that not everyone experiences same-sex attraction in the same way.

This is all very useful to talk about sexual attraction, but what of emotional needs? I've seen no scale to measure the need to connect emotionally with one's own sex, but I imagine that need varies widely too. Mine is very strong; that I'm not a six on Kinsey's scale is a major indicator that the emotional need is distinct from physical attraction.

Apart from sex, there's an important lesson here: Healthful same-sex emotional interaction can be very fulfilling, yet emotional needs can *manifest* as sexual desire (regardless of sexual orientation). Have you ever thought you were hungry when you were actually dehydrated? If your need is water, eating more is never going to satisfy your thirst. Similarly, if we have long suppressed our need for emotional connection with those our own sex, it is possible to go overboard in pursuit of affection and get involved sexually. Just as food can't satisfy thirst, sex will never satisfy emotional deficits.

Unfortunately, a lot of people are unaware of the distinction between legitimate emotional need and the sex drive.[7] To exacerbate the situation, many of us have had unfortunate experiences that caused us to confuse sexual and emotional involvement. Others have been pursued romantically in extreme ways (or, at least, against their wills or protestations), so, sadly, a lot of people have learned to be emotionally *un*available.

Now that I am aware of a real need to connect *emotionally* with those of my sex and I've been relating with men in warm, healthful ways, my emotional needs are being satisfied, so sex with men is no longer the enticement for me that it used to be. It's been helpful to realize that "healthful ways" doesn't necessarily mean at arms' length. Just as our attractions to others differs, so too do the healthful solutions to meeting our emotional needs differ. Your own emotional needs and how to meet them may be different than mine.

For married people, it's important to remember that couples may be best served by encouraging their spouses (straight, gay, bi, or other) to meet legitimate same-sex *emotional* needs in healthful ways. Invite your spouse to have healthy friendships. Some guys are content to play ball together; some of us talk, share feelings, and hug. For those of us with strong same-sex emotional needs, these activities are vital.[8]

Meeting connection needs healthfully and regularly, with no sexual agenda, can illuminate our true needs to us, open previously unimagined relational possibilities, and greatly diminish selfish or unhealthful impulses toward others. It might also help with addictive behavior, reducing the draw of gaming, spending, pornography, or overeating, because the emptiness that was there is now filled with satisfying human connection.

There's an elephant in the room: Sex feels very good. Sexual connection is satisfying while it lasts. What if you don't want sexual urges toward those of your sex to diminish? My sense is that people, generally, do want *something* better than a self-focused yearning: deep, lasting connection (the process toward which I cover in coming chapters). I suspect our culture is, generally, overfocused on sex due to deficits in other kinds of connection and because the intensity of sex *seems* like a quick and easy fix.[9]

Don't take this as suggestion that establishing emotional connections with one's own sex erases physical attraction—not at all! But when tempered by emotional satisfaction, sexual desire becomes less of a taskmaster and more of a lens to better understand and foster satisfying relationships. I used to want my attraction to men to go away—now, I see it as a gift that opens doors to deeply fulfilling relationships.

It's understandable if you're apprehensive about trying a new approach. Proceed with some caution, but definitely proceed. If you feel physical attraction to people of your sex, it's possible to vet people of your sex and determine who would be safe to share thoughts, feelings, or affection with without obscuring (via sex) the deepest *relating*. It is also on you to establish and articulate healthful boundaries in *all* your relationships.[10]

Those who understand that emotional and social needs are real and ongoing grasp that meeting those needs healthfully rather than ignoring them can strengthen *all* relationships, even "traditional" marriage. Heck, it increases enjoyment of *every* good thing in life![11]

POINTS TO PONDER

- Nowhere in this book do I say that sex is inherently bad—nor do I say that gay sex fulfills emotional need or leads to the deepest lasting connection.

- Legitimate needs can be met healthfully—but not removed. Same-sex *emotional* needs are real and *ongoing.* They must not be neglected. What benefit might there be in having to figure out needs that aren't readily obvious?

- Emotional needs *can* appear as sexual desire, like feeling hungry when you're dehydrated. Can you think of habits or behaviors in your own life that aren't satisfying you in the ways you hope?

- Meeting emotional needs healthfully can illuminate true needs, open previously unimagined relational possibilities, and diminish selfish or unhealthful impulses toward others. It might also reduce compulsive behavior. What specific benefits have you seen when emotional needs are met?

NOTES

1. "No man is an island entire of itself. Every man is a piece of the continent, a part of the main." John Donne, *Devotions Upon Emergent Occasions* (London: Vintage, 1623) Ch. 17. See Jesse Johnson, "Why Men Need Other Men to Prosper," Vital Collective, n.d., https://vitalcollective.com/why-men-need-other-men-to-prosper/; Paul Friesen, "4 Things Men Need from Other Men (That They Can't Get from Women,"

Biola University Center for Marriage and Relationships, January 29, 2019, https://cmr.biola.edu/blog/2019/jan/29/4-things-men-need-other-men-they-cant-get-women/; Wednesday Lee Friday, "Women Are Often More Lonely Than We Let On," The Roots of Loneliness Project, 2022, accessed August 21, 2022, https://www.rootsofloneliness.com/lonely-women.

2. My sense is that the invention of the word *homosexual* has done severe damage to individuals and to society as a whole; it narrows all same-sex love down to one definition that denotes sexual expression. However, simple attraction to—a desire to be with—those of one's own sex has historically had an abundance of meanings and feelings for most people. Even when there has been intense love expressed between persons of the same sex, not all of them desired or expressed that love sexually. Most healthy people have some kind of attraction to their own sex, and these attractions have a variety of impetuses and manifestations. Linking sexual expression to the entire spectrum of same-sex attractions can cause bewilderment and self-doubt while also bringing outsider condemnation on "moral" grounds. See "How and When the Word Homosexual Was First Introduced into the Bible," Canyon Walker Connections (blog), November 25, 2017, https://canyonwalkerconnections.com/word-homosexual-first-introduced-bible/; Robert P. George, "The Philosophical Basis of Biblical Marriage," *Public Square Magazine*, January 6, 2022, https://publicsquaremag.org/faith/gospel-fare/the-philosophical-basis-of-biblical-marriage/.

3. Cultural norms can hold us back or inform us. I remember standing next to one of the "Lost Boys" (Sudanese refugee) for some photographs to be taken; though we had barely met, he instinctively took my hand. Such behavior—including men kissing or walking arm in arm with men in some countries—has nothing to do with homosexuality but with natural affection. (A kiss between men in many cultures signifies neither an exclusive nor a sexual pairing.)

4. Nothing will eliminate my legitimate need to connect healthfully with men.

5. Rather than take (or threaten to take) what brings an addict joy and connection, increase healthful versions of it! See American Addiction Institute, "Understanding the Root Cause of Addiction," American Institute of Mind and Medicine, 2020, https://american-addiction.com/lapse-vs-relapse/.

6. Kinsey Institute, "The Kinsey Scale," Indiana University, 2020, https://kinseyinstitute.org/research/publications/kinsey-scale.php. Newer, more detailed sexual orientation scales exist; this book uses Kinsey's for simplicity and familiarity. I acknowledge that even gender identity has complex biological and psychological nuances, but for simplicity in describing sexual orientation, I use basic male/female attractions here. Some people confuse same-sex attraction with pedophilia. I and most LGBTQIA and heterosexual people are not attracted to children. See Ian Johnston, "Pedophilia a 'Sexual Orientation—Like Being Straight or Gay,'" *Independent*, April 3, 2016, https://www.independent.co.uk/news/paedophilia-sexual-orientation-straight-gay-criminal-psychologist-child-sex-abuse-a6965956.html. Regarding options,

David A. Bednar says, "When we define ourselves by the labels of the world, we limit our divine potential and, in so doing, limit our ability to choose." "And Nothing Shall Offend Them," *Ensign*, November 2006, 89–92.

7. See chapter 8; Nazanin Moali, "Men, Arousal, and Erections: Why They Don't Always Come Together," Oasis2Care, last updated December 18, 2019, https://oasis2care.com/sexuality/men-arousal-and-erections-why-they-dont-always-come-together/; Go Ask Alice, "Can Erections Happen When You're Not Sexually Aroused," Columbia University, last updated April 30, 2015, https://goaskalice.columbia.edu/answered-questions/can-erections-happen-when-youre-not-sexually-aroused; McGill, "I May Have an Erection but I'm Just Not That Into It," *McGill University News and Events*, last updated July 23, 2013, https://www.mcgill.ca/channels/news/i-may-have-erection-i%E2%80%99m-just-not-it-229207; "Is an Erection Always an Indication of a Sexual Arousal or Attraction? Why or Why Not?" Quora, n.d., https://www.quora.com/Is-an-erection-always-an-indication-of-a-sexual-arousal-or-attraction-Why-or-why-not.

8. See Morton Hunt, "About Men; The Comfort of Pals," *The New York Times*, January 18, 1987, https://www.nytimes.com/1987/01/18/magazine/about-men-the-comfort-of-pals.html.

9. See Lewis, *The Four Loves*, 57–91.

10. I must state that, at least for an addict, no rule, no boundary—no risk of jail, HIV, death by a psychopath, public humiliation, family destruction, loss of employment and everything and everyone—is sufficient deterrent to acting out or "using." To quote the experts, addiction is "cunning,

baffling, and powerful." *Sexaholics Anonymous* ("White Book," Brentwood, TN: Sexaholics Anonymous, 1984), 2. It's no fiction that the astounding intellect of Dr. Arthur C. Doyle's fictional character Sherlock Holmes was no match against his own opioid addiction (you likely know real-life examples). How is it that I don't want my "drug of choice" today? Grace and the superior connections that actually meet my needs (see chapters 8 – 9).

11. See Chantelle Pattemore, "How to Set Boundaries in Your Relationships," Psych Central (blog), last updated June 3, 2021, https://psychcentral.com/blog/why-healthy-relationships-always-have-boundaries-how-to-set-boundaries-in-yours. On ongoing emotional need: "She does not realise that the husband whom she succeeds in isolating from his own kind will not be very well worth having." Lewis, *The Four Loves*, 15, 76. See also Matt Walsh, "The Most Effective Way to Destroy Your Husband, Ruin Your Marriage, and Encourage Infidelity," *The Daily Wire*, n.d., https://www.dailywire.com/news/walsh-most-effective-way-destroy-your-husband-ruin-matt-walsh.

CHAPTER 5

Is Fluidity Real?—Are Feelings Forever?

Some choices are binary, with only two options: breathe or suffocate, eat or starve, sleep or try to stay awake. But most choices present multiple options; we are only limited in our choices by our ability to see alternatives. For a very long time, I could only see "limited" options!

B Y PRESENTING MULTIPLE PATHS, I DON'T mean to imply that each is equally desirable—or that all paths are harmless. The natural consequences of what we choose can limit us physically or materially or spiritually; for example, people aware of our poor choices are less likely to trust us with things or opportunities, and we can even lose our liberty via incarceration or to chemical dependence or other addictions. Poor choices often reduce future choices.

I have known my share of addicts. What surprises me is how often *nonaddicts* express doubt about a loss of free will in addiction. Whether a physiological process actually retards cognitive ability or whether addiction can only be described as psychological chains, I know that at one point in my life, I personally experienced a significant reduction in my ability to choose actions against feeding my compulsion. One person's ability to "control" their own appetite for alcohol (or food or drugs or sex) doesn't mean that another person has the same ability—or that the first person will always be able to maintain that level of control.[1]

When you've limited your options through poor choices, moving forward is like trying to climb out of a hole with inadequate tools: It's slow at best. For me, there was no instant fix to compulsive behavior. I have the responsibility of studying my situation and discovering who I am and what is best for me. Then, I sincerely follow the "steps" I've established to reach my objectives (though I don't believe anyone does it on their own).

The twelve steps of Alcoholics Anonymous have been invaluable in helping me receive power I clearly did not possess (in AA, we refer to it as a Higher Power, and it doesn't necessarily mean God; for some it can be one's group of fellow addicts). I am talking here about power over compulsive behavior—not same-sex attraction. I am grateful for the gift of same-sex attraction. (There is something more powerful than the twelve steps for anything you face, which I'll share in another chapter.)

As I shared my feelings, thoughts, and deeds with other people, my compulsive sexual activity diminished. It was possible to actually say no. My social interactions became more nurturing. Interestingly, my own efforts weren't making these changes; I had tried willpower and anything else I could think of, without success. Instead, my steps were a mere demonstration that I sincerely wanted power beyond my own.

Sometimes I thought I was cured of my compulsions, and I'd stop working the twelve steps, slacking off on calling and meeting group members, only to relapse.[2] Part of my path includes rules to help me avoid relapse, because I know I'm not smarter than my addiction. Some of my early rules were unrealistic; for example, I forbid myself from being alone with another man with same-sex attraction (as if that were a detail I'd always know!). It wasn't that I didn't trust them; I didn't trust me.

Though shortsighted and sometimes hurtful to others, these rules were all I could come up with at the time. What I really needed was *increased* interaction with men who were unafraid of real connection, but at the time, I couldn't see many ways for that to happen, considering my compulsive history.

Of note, while I'd come very close to marrying women on multiple occasions, I don't think I have seriously entertained, at least not as a mature adult, the idea that I would, in this life, "change" to a heterosexual. That is, I haven't viewed marriage to a woman as a "cure" for my same-sex attraction.

Still, we can imagine how disillusioned, discouraged, and even angry a person might feel if they were persuaded, by self or another person, that physical attraction to one's sex vanishes in mortality, only to fall maddeningly short of that goal or believe they'd achieved it and then "relapse." I can't judge anyone or their desires, but I wouldn't condone promising someone that it's likely they'll become heterosexual in this life. That said, I can see how someone who has experienced an ebb and flow of attraction for same and opposite sex, as I have, might persuasively tell themselves, "I am now heterosexual." I suspect it's more likely that they currently feel more heterosexual than gay. Some queer people never experience this, but fluidity in attraction is not unusual.[3]

IS *CHANGE* AN OFFENSIVE WORD?

Though not alcoholic, I've been in AA meetings, and I know how maddening it might be for the usual addict to hear someone say, "One day, God took away my desire to drink, and I've never wanted a drop since." Yet, this sometimes is heard in AA meetings, and I believe people have experienced this.

Again, while my sense is that most people attracted to their own sex are attracted for wonderful reasons, which won't likely go away in one's lifetime, my own experience is that whom one is attracted to *can* be fluid. (It's important to remember that physical attraction alone is a poor basis for any relationship.)[4]

Personally, I don't believe our need to foster relationships with those of our *own* sex will ever disappear (thank heaven!), nor do I believe people will eternally want sexual relationships with their sex. My views aren't solely a result of my experience with fluidity but are also products of reason and precedent: I've experienced significant changes already going from entrenched sex addiction to more healthful relating with both sexes. [5]

POINTS TO PONDER

- As you read, you may see that your journey, or your loved one's, is similar to mine. You'll also see some differences, maybe significant ones. What can you learn from the similarities and differences in our experiences?
- By presenting multiple paths, I don't mean to imply that each is equally desirable—or that all are harmless. How have your choices taught you this?
- How can differences enrich us?
- People attracted to their own sex will likely remain so attracted in their lifetime for wonderful purposes.

NOTES

1. See Denise Cummins, "The Myth and Reality of Free Will: The Case of Addiction," Psychology Today (blog), February 9, 2014, https://www.psychologytoday.com/us/blog/good-thinking/201402/the-myth-and-reality-free-will-the-case-addiction.

2. I was never addicted to alcohol, but when I first moved to Utah, I had trouble locating a twelve-step meeting for sex addicts, so I attended AA. (My responses to inquiries about my "drug of choice" were entertaining!)

3. "What Does Sexually Fluid Mean?" Web MD, November 27, 2021, https://www.webmd.com/sex-relationships/what-does-sexually-fluid-mean. See also "Can Sexuality Change? What Sexual Fluidity Is and Is Not," Good Therapy (blog), June 24, 2018, https://www.goodtherapy.org/blog/can-sexuality-change-what-sexual-fluidity-is-and-is-not-0624187/amp/.

4. My experience with fluid attraction informs me that people are creatures of change—though no change can be permanently forced on anyone. As a side note, over my lifetime, my attraction to women and men has evolved in satisfying ways. (I think people's grasp of some fluidity in their own lives is at the heart of much homophobia.) Martin Luther King Jr. famously said, "People fail to get along because they fear each other; they fear each other because they don't know each other; they don't know each other because they have not communicated with each other."

5. Evaluate your own changes—and those of people you know. While you personally may never have experienced changes in attraction, you likely know someone like me—and you likely have experienced other kinds of changes. I used to hate pumpkin pie; I *love* it now! I used to love board games; not much now. I thought I didn't like sci-fi movies—then I saw *Star Wars*. As a young man, I believed I could never be a physical threat to anyone; but just observe me if someone puts my loved ones in peril. We are all on a spectrum, a continuum of metamorphoses. While no one is static or

cemented into a slot. I don't believe it's healthful to hide one's feelings, nor do I believe it's likely a gay person will become heterosexual in this life.

CHAPTER 6

The Paradox of Sex

"Love ceases to be a demon only when he ceases to be a god."[1]

—M. Denis de Rougemont

NOTE THAT *EROS* IN THESE PASSAGES from C. S. Lewis means classical love and not eroticism:

> Others, with Eros [love] as their fuel and also as their model, can embark on the married life, within which Eros, of himself, will never be enough—will indeed survive only in so far as he is continually chastened and corroborated by higher principles.
>
> But Eros honoured without reservation and obeyed unconditionally, becomes a demon. And this is just how he claims to be honoured and obeyed. Divinely indifferent to our selfishness, he is also demoniacally rebellious to every claim of God or Man that would oppose him. Hence, as the poet says: "People in love cannot be moved by kindness, and opposition makes them feel like martyrs."[2]

EUPHORIA

I'm now going to address the misconception that same-sex attraction presents a binary choice: either suppress your feelings and remain alone or embrace a fully sexualized gay life. To avoid missing empowering insights, I encourage you to read this chapter in one sitting. Pardon that much of this comes from the male point of view; it's the only one I have.

I believe that sex (or mutual activities that tend to result in sexual climax) opens not only the heart but also the psyche, the soul. Sex can be a transcendent, bonding thing. I acknowledge that male-female sex may not currently be that—even for some heterosexual people.

Non-bonding sex *also* opens the psyche . . . to other outcomes. I want to be clear: I am convinced that some sex is sex that opens the psyche/soul to negative influences and outcomes. This can be so in cisgender heterosexual relations—even in heterosexual married sex! I *don't* believe sex is only for procreation, but some sex is not mutually agreed on, appropriate, or cherished by both participants, and it's detrimental to the intimacy of the relationship.

Can "inappropriate" sex feel good? Absolutely—intensely so. Still, what some call "love" is temporary sexual euphoria. Euphoria is a transitory feeling within the self; it is not connection with another. While it might accompany love, euphoria is *not* love.[3] There is danger of real tragedy in confusing euphoria for love—also in exalting even true love above anything else. C. S. Lewis wrote:

Of all loves [Eros] is, at his height, most god-like; therefore most prone to demand our worship. Of himself he always tends to turn "being in love" into a sort of religion. . . .

"Love made us do it," notice the tone. A man saying "I did it because I was frightened," or "I did it because I was angry," speaks quite differently. . . . But lovers are seldom doing quite that. Notice how tremulously, almost how devoutly, they say the word *love*, not so much pleading in an "extenuating circumstance" as appealing to an authority. The confession can be almost a boast. There can be a shade of defiance in it. They "feel like martyrs." In extreme cases what their words really express is a demure yet unshakable allegiance to the god of love. They are now under a new law. . . . The "spirit" of Eros supersedes all laws, and they must not [offend] it. . . .

It seems to sanction all sorts of actions they would not otherwise have dared. I do not mean solely, or chiefly, acts that violate chastity. They are just as likely to be acts of injustice or uncharity against the outer world. They will seem like proofs of piety and zeal towards Eros. The pair can say to one another in an almost sacrificial spirit, "It is for love's sake that I have neglected my parents—left my children—cheated my partner—failed my friend at his greatest need." These reasons in love's law have passed for good. The [devotees] may even come to feel a particular merit in such sacrifices; what costlier offering can be laid on love's altar than one's own conscience?[4]

Apart from the harm that comes from exalting true love above all other considerations, confusing transitory euphoria for love can be a step toward falling out of "love" due to the fleeting nature of euphoria. I say this having repeatedly experienced emptiness and pain by opening my soul to negative outcomes. Here, I am *not* speaking of cultural guilt from my upbringing; before I ever felt any guilt or shame from my religion over my sexual activity, I had already experienced the hollowness that follows transitory sexual euphoria. I was not taught that premarital *or* gay sex could hurt before I began acting sexually; I didn't even know what sex was at the time, but I experienced the natural letdown and ache all the same.

Something to contemplate: Sex can be an instrument of profound bonding; *any* other use of sex seems to lead to disappointment, if not harm—heterosexual or gay or other. Nobody wants their loved ones to suffer these negative influences and non-bonding outcomes. This is why we should never encourage sexual relations we don't personally know are healthful long-term.[5]

MORE IS NOT MORE

I've known *a lot* of gay men!

I've experienced firsthand euphoric excitement with men. The biggest puzzle for me has been that sex between men doesn't seem to bond a pair to the same depth and duration as non-sexual gay couples and some opposite-sex couples (certainly not *all* heterosexual couples). I'm not saying that lasting connection doesn't exist between people of the same sex, only that when it happens, it seems to happen a different way than with bonded heterosexual couples. I don't pretend to know why same sex couples (apparently) experience the deepest, lasting weld non-sexually and some straight couples experience that depth sexually; my working theory is that men and women can bond sexually long-term because they are sufficiently dissimilar.[6]

While exhilarating (sometimes electric!), sexual stimulation between men seems to lead to emotional distancing—though, at first, it feels like connection. Euphoria can last for days. I think men often do establish true emotional connection with each other; then, based on the more-is-more fallacy, they get sexual and, evidently, erode the linkage. I have experienced this again and again. Some men openly acknowledge that they use sex to *avoid* intimacy.[7]

PAIRING PATHS

Many gay men remain bewildered by the lack of deep union between themselves and their significant others. A lot of couples remain silent, thinking they are the anomaly among many happy gay pairs, but they are like other sexual gay partners: connected only to a point. In my observation, even gay married couples in the first weeks of sexual euphoria (much mistaken for love) seem to crash into the reality of separateness, unless (ironically) they stop being sexual and nourish the unique bonding expressions of infinite same-sex connection. Many gay couples have discovered this key.

My friend Mica from California never acted sexually with men in his first thirty-five years of life because he grew up in a tight group of buddies that camped, played, and hung out together. It was much like the comradery that nourished my same-sex emotional needs while I was a missionary for two years. These close male connections met his true needs until they married off and became busy with families. After moving to Utah—even farther from that nourishment—Mica had some euphoric gay trysts, then married a man. Only *weeks* into his marriage, he acknowledged that the flame between him and his husband was already gone.

Of course, there are many unhappy heterosexual couples and many who have divorced: Wedded bliss is elusive for both heterosexuals and gays. Yet, the lack of deep union that can occur with heterosexual married couples seems universal (by my observations) between people whose sexual acts by nature open the soul to negative outcomes—straight, gay, or otherwise—in what one might otherwise expect to be a very intimate link. Though the chasm need not be irreparable.

There is one caveat: Dependence or overreliance on euphoria can give the *illusion* of connectedness, making a person feel they have a deep union with another—and making them quite reluctant to give up sexual relating. (It can be excruciatingly difficult, at least, in the first days of euphoria.) Have you ever done something to a partner that you knew they wouldn't like, but you felt it was too exciting to resist? Expressions preceded by "Just let me . . ." are often a red flag that your gratification—not love—is your motivation. Your "bond" may actually be dependence on the high of orgasm. Self-focused gratification can increase personal appetites in a compounding way that never satisfies. Wanting more always leads to wanting more. Many guys who believed they had a good bond with a partner were surprised to find themselves acting sexually with another person (their true same-sex needs weren't being met—by the partner or in the tryst).

Some couples, gay and heterosexual, resort to novel sexual experiences in an attempt to strengthen their bond. In the past, I have been invited into "marital activities" by gay couples. They didn't appear to be into each other much and seemed to hope to preserve the union by adding me to mix. Good as it is, sexual euphoria can't fulfill real emotional need, and euphoria doesn't last—which is why so many guys with partners seek outside guys; they think they've lost love when it is actually euphoria that has faded. All the while, the soul continues to crave true same-sex connection.

But giving up a partner isn't always necessary (unless that person is unwilling to contemplate nonsexual options). My friend Jaime and his male partner have been together for more than sixteen years—and they're deeply united in love. They haven't been sexual with each other for many years, and neither seems interested in pairing with anyone else. I'm convinced that their relationship has lasted not in spite of ending the sex, but *because* of it: They've grown into a deeper connection than what sex brought them, and their bond is no longer threatened by the post-euphoria distancing of same-sex sex.

If you know of a gay couple wherein both partners still genuinely cherish each other—prefer each other's company over all other options after twenty or so years—I would wager they are no longer being sexual, though they more than likely reinforce their union with affection.

Pardon the metaphor, but same-sex touch is like rubbing alcohol: so soothing on the skin, not so great taken internally! True lasting connection is heavenly. When we try to deepen it with orgasms, there's euphoria for a bit, then an isolating ache, as from ingesting something intended to soothe topically (or, at least, pervasive emotional thirst). As with street drugs, people seek more of what makes them sick—euphoria or specious connection—even from strangers; you might want this, as I did, if your "hits" have included sexual stimulation (calories instead of hydration). The relationships around you and me seem to bear this out.

Our gay friends' blissful posts on social media only show the electric euphoria, never the letdowns and putting themselves on the market again and again, chasing fulfillment of legitimate emotional needs in a wasteland of sex—apparently missing the deepest connection via sexual relating. Even for people who put off sex until they are in love, it appears that same-sex sexual behavior interferes with enduring bonds.

I'm not persuaded that gay sexual partnerships fail because of societal disapproval. I grew up in the San Francisco Bay Area; not only was "free love" preached there all my years, but so was gay life. Some Bible Belt communities may have condemned gayness regularly, but that hasn't been the norm in my California turf for some time. Even in that tolerant environment, I observed that even exclusive gay partnerships that didn't discover nonsexual bonding tended to fizzle out (as did most "open" partnerships).

Many gay couples, some together for decades, have made accommodations driven by the quest for ongoing euphoria by opening up their marriages or overlooking cheating. By contrast, I personally know multiple happy gay couples that are no longer sexual, yet they have been bonded for a decade or more.

I'm not declaring that one hundred percent of sexual gay partnerships fail as far as monogamy or union (though it wouldn't surprise me), but I ask—rhetorically—what have you observed? Is the long-term happy couple you know faithful and sexual, or might they now be enjoying something better than gay sex? How united are those in open marriages? My point isn't to prove or disprove the existence of a long-term faithful and sexual gay couple. The important question for a great many of us is this: Even if a gay couple exists that is happily monogamous and sexual for twenty or so years, given the scarcity of examples, might the nonsexual cases I've cited, and my coming suggestions for lasting same-sex fulfillment, be well founded and worth your time?

I know firsthand the lack of fulfillment many of us have experienced while trying to establish same-sex bonds sexually, so I cannot sincerely congratulate anyone entering such a partnership. I will wish couples every happiness, but internally, I don't celebrate something that, I've observed, keeps people from deeper union.

Some people have told me, "You just haven't had sex with the right man," or "You weren't in love." I'm not saying men can't love other men, because I certainly do, nor am I saying there is no pleasure or euphoria in gay sex, only that there seems to be something in that sex that holds people away from the deeper connection we're seeking. More importantly, there's something elevated in nonsexual same-sex welds that promotes and reinforces lasting relations. It took me years to put my finger on the difference, but it all comes back to shedding the gradual—or immediate—post-euphoric stupor (thirst/emptiness) I've described above and choosing a bond that can be limitless in depth and duration. I'm discussing outcomes that are not necessarily externally imposed: equal and opposite reactions we can only temporarily ignore. Some are obvious; some take time to appreciate.

Today, I enjoy profound, lasting male connection. In coming chapters, I'll detail how to create enduring union with someone/people of one's own sex.

While I have poignant personal feelings on sexual gay unions, I've rarely dissuaded persons who are determined to be sexual with those of their sex—though I will share my experience if asked (sometimes when I am not asked). For some of us, there is no other way to comprehend or be persuaded about something than to experience it (hopefully not on perpetual replay). I know that no damage need be permanent (see chapter 5), though we might miss out on some blessings as we stubbornly struggle to learn from our own experiences.

Can same-sex links be repaired? Yes. People of the same sex, regardless of sexual orientation, are designed to love each other powerfully and in distinct ways from opposite-sex pairings. Same-sex unity, limited by sex, can be repaired by embracing the unique same-sex bonding that meets legitimate needs, the (often overlooked) expressions that facilitate the deepest, most resilient same-sex connection.

SACRED COW

Though I'm not an authority on bonding in heterosexual marriages, I've observed some similarities and differences with same-sex couples. When I say that some heterosexual couples find lasting connection sexually and people of the same sex find it in nonsexual ways, my naive impression is that those heterosexual pairs seem to stumble into union by chance. (I really don't know how it happens—it seems random to me. Even when both partners work hard at the marriage, only some of them bond.) I've happily observed that people of the same sex—regardless of orientation— appear to be *wired* with the potential for deep union with each other (even if they also enjoy a spousal relationship with someone of the opposite sex).

In many cultures, sex isn't the highest expression of love. Many heterosexual couples will affirm that sex does not necessarily equate to intimacy and that unity—not sex—is the top benefit to their relationship.[9]

Overall, I challenge society's sacred cow of sex. I've had many sexual experiences, and I've lived decades without sex. I disagree that nothing is better than sex, that one cannot survive without sex, and I disagree that the ultimate expression of love is sex.[10]

IS SEX A NEED?

Imagine you're indefinitely stuck halfway down a hole, unable to reach anything below your waist (yet you can urinate and defecate). Within reach is all the food and water you'll ever need. Will you perish from deprivation of any sort? Nope. While you might experience great yearning—even torment yourself in the first couple years that you're going crazy or dying from lack of sex—you'd soon learn it isn't so. This scenario is unappealing (thank heaven most of us can move about!), but it illustrates that your greatest deprivation would be psychological—if you were deprived of human social relating.

My point is that our social needs are critical. Sex is wonderful (and a want). Emotional connections are a need, and only when bonding needs are met can human relations be truly understood and valued.

Loving someone doesn't always mean it's best to be sexual with that person (it may not be good for you or for the other person).[11] Married heterosexual people still need to control physical appetites, free-love advocates can't have sex whenever they want, and even the uber-wealthy discover that they can't have all they want whenever they want it. Some of the most difficult trials for heterosexual people through history also involve not being with the person they most loved—and many of the most satisfying relationships were never sexual.

Some people sabotage real connectedness by presuming that any kind of love expression, or escalation of expression, increases or deepens their connection. There are love expressions that build bonds between mother and daughter, friends, siblings, father and son, husband and wife, and so on, expressions that—in one scenario—build connection, yet the same expressions might *diminish* bonding in other situations. Disciplining our desires and love expressions appropriately allows us to cherish our various relationships.[12]

Some people have expressed pity that I currently don't experience sexual expression with someone. Some have intimated to me that perhaps I'm in denial about my desires and need to own them; this suggestion implies that I haven't tried their way of living and presumes that I haven't explored my feelings. These opinions can be surprising for me to hear; after nearly five decades of contemplating my attractions and varied relations, I've encountered a path that fulfills me more than gay sexual relationships ever did—this seems like considerable rumination. As good as orgasm can be, I pity those who've never experienced deep, abiding union because their fixation on sexual euphoria has prevented them from progressing to deeper human connection.

My own experience tells me that sexuality (and, I suspect, gender identity) can be fluid. What may repel you today *might* actually attract you in some future era.

Regardless, romantic "love" isn't optimal relating for couples of any orientation—even sexual expression can't hold a candle to lasting, immutable union. Isn't much of the pain we experience in our lives the result of comparison and unrealistic expectations? Life is too short to waste on needless anguish.[13] If you don't want an opposite-sex partner, you have other wondrous relationship options here and now![14]

I appeal to the expert on you: *you*. Look back over your life and honestly assess your emotions and relationships. Taking all feelings into account (not just sexual euphoria), over the long run, how bonded have you remained to persons of your sex with whom you continue to be sexual? Perhaps take some weeks or months to come to a conclusion and an opinion for yourself on the odds for long-term same-sex bonding (sexual versus nonsexual). Even if you and the most important person in your life were sexual in the past, perhaps you're now enjoying the lasting nonsexual ties I speak of.

I've learned that resilient, fulfilling relationships are not just for a few heterosexual couples. Just about anyone can find union. My deepest, most rewarding relationships resulted from the loss of relations and unmet expectations that I previously held as important (I now feel that I've experienced deeper connection than most heterosexuals). Your best relationships may not be the one(s) you're currently in or pursuing or think you're missing out on (or they may not come about in the way you're trying to build them). I suspect that many more women (straight, lesbian, and queer) and heterosexual men have experienced the same-sex bonding joys I'm discussing than have gay men (a big reason I wrote this book is because *I* was long distracted from these insights by orgasm).[14] There are more factors for your consideration ahead; ultimately, you must be the judge.

POINTS TO PONDER

- Everyone has multiple human relation options. Your most rewarding relationships may not be the ones you think you're missing. Seeing abundant options might require modification to current notions. It's possible that the person you have the deepest connection to forever is the same sex as you.

- Emotional connection is a need. Sex is not love and doesn't satisfy true needs. Confusing euphoria for love often leads to falling out of "love" due to the fleeting nature of the emotion. How else have you found emotional connections in your relationships?

- Inappropriate or selfish sex—heterosexual or otherwise—disconnects us from the joy of union (and can be torture to escape; wanting more always leads to wanting more). In particular, sexual stimulation between people of the same sex can prevent the deepest emotional bonds—even for those who wait until they're in love. How might this effort to create a bond sexually have the opposite effect?

- Many have experienced the profound connection that can endure between people of the same sex who *avoid* being sexual with each other. Same-sex bonds can be repaired/deepened. There are happy gay couples who are not sexual yet are truly united for decades. What other welds might be at work in these relationships?

NOTES

1. "Love ceases to be a demon only when it ceases to be a god." M. Denis de Rougemont, RightWords.eu, YourCHOICE, accessed August 19, 2022, https://rightwords.eu/quotes/love-ceases-to-be-a-demon-only-when-it-ceases-to-be-a-god--31669.

2. Lewis, *The Four Loves*, 6.

3. Euphoria is a sense of pleasure—even temporary joy—like a drug high. Because it is chemically induced, it cannot last. I've lost count of the sexually partnered gay men I've met who are no longer experiencing the euphoria they called

"love." See also *Merriam-Webster.com Dictionary*, s.v. "euphoria," accessed August 8, 2022, https://www.merriam-webster.com/dictionary/euphoria.

4. "And all the time the grim joke is that this Eros whose voice seems to speak from the eternal realm is not himself necessarily even permanent. He is notoriously the most mortal of our loves. . . . Our natural loves [are] rivals to the love of God. . . . When God arrives (and only then) the half-gods can [take their proper places]. Left to themselves they either vanish or become demons. Only in His name can they with beauty and security 'wield their little tridents.' The rebellious slogan 'All for love' is really love's death warrant." Lewis, *The Four Loves*, 92, 110–15, 118–19.

5. Please see Epilogue.

6. Could it be possible that oxytocin, the feel-good/bonding hormone released in cuddling and sex, doesn't seem to affect same-sex couples in the same ways it affects heterosexual couples? My experience is that feeling good happens for both, but bonding, not so much with same-sex sex. I believe that something other than chemical reaction is going on. See also Stephanie Watson, "Oxytocin: The Love Hormone," Harvard Health Publishing, July 20, 2021, https://www.health.harvard.edu/mind-and-mood/oxytocin-the-love-hormone.

7. One definition of *intimacy* is "belonging to or characterizing one's deepest nature." *Merriam-Webster.com Dictionary*, s.v. "intimacy," accessed August 8, 2022, https://www.merriam-webster.com/dictionary/intimate.

8. See "Newton's Laws of Motion," Glenn Research Center, last updated June 30, 2022, https://www1.grc.nasa.gov/beginners-guide-to-aeronautics/newtons-laws-of-motion/;

God didn't invent consequence/justice. H. Donl Peterson, "The Law of Justice and the Law of Mercy" in *The Book of Mormon: Alma, the Testimony of the Word*, ed. Monte S. Nyman and Charles D. Tate Jr. (Provo, UT: Religious Studies Center, Brigham Young University, 1992), 211–22, https://rsc.byu.edu/book-mormon-alma-testimony-word/ law-justice-law-mercy.

9. Family life professor Stephen F. Duncan cites the National Health and Social Life Survey: "About 20 percent of [heterosexual] couples at any age have a nonsexual marriage." M. Sue Bergin, "Don't Let Your Marriage Go Cold," *BYU Magazine*, March 2020, https://magazine.byu.edu/article/ dont-let-your-marriage-go-cold/. And it's not necessarily a bad thing: See Jennifer Harbutt, "'I Don't Think We'll Ever Have Sex Again': Our Happy, Cuddly, Celibate Marriage," *The Guardian*, April 15, 2017, https://www.theguardian. com/lifeandstyle/2017/apr/15/celibate-marriage-sex-sex-less-relationship. See also Edward O. Laumann et al., "National Health and Social Life Survey, 1992: [United States]," Inter-university Consortium for Political and Social Research (April 17, 2008), https://doi.org/10.3886/ ICPSR06647.v2.

10. "Greater love hath no man than this, that a man lay down his life for his friends." Bible, John 15:12–13.

11. Jails and hospitals have a number of people in them who at some point presumed that *any* expression of love in any scenario is only a positive thing. Many people are hooked on the *idea* of sex with a particular person. Real life, films, and fiction are filled with examples of relationship tragedy— not because society created the consequences but because

mistrust, neglect, depression, and jealousy are natural consequences of infidelity.

12. Ask several people about the person they were or are closest to and (if they're comfortable saying) whether it was a sexual relationship. This can be an illuminating exercise.

13. Some people mistakenly believe those with physical or mental limitations, the widowed, or the aged may not have a sex drive. It's also untrue that every married person is content, with all their sexual and intimate needs met. I'm not saying same-sex attraction is no worse or somehow better than another situation (often I am saying that last part!), only that each of us has unique circumstances that might puzzle us. "I'm not sure *anyone* lives in that perfect, ideal family. . . . My own experiences have sometimes brought me bright pain and concentrated loneliness. It's easy to blame that pain on the category of my life circumstances, but I've come to see that everyone is dealing with pain. . . . It's the state of mortality. The best we can do is try to help bear each other's pain." Sharon Eubank, "A Letter to a Single Sister," *Ensign*, March 2020, 40–41.

14. Some people's decisions are harder than others; still, I think everyone will, in the end, acknowledge that their circumstances facilitated the best opportunities for growth and self-discovery (unfolding happiness). Being true to one's heart should never mean abandoning facts. Relationships (simply) based on emotion tend to be disjointed, dysfunctional, and fragile, as opposed to those based on character and commitment, where devotion is to the *union*, not primarily to the partner (more disciplined, yet with a better success rate; unwavering commitment to the *partner* may not be possible on all days).

CHAPTER 7

Beyond Grief—What If I Don't Have Support?

The appendixes of this book have excellent resources for LGBTQIA persons and those that love them. For perspective, I'm including some personal events that taught me that the loss of some things we hold dear can open us to receiving far better things.

AS YEARS PASSED AFTER MY MISSION, my stomach distress worsened, becoming constant and painful; it seemed whatever I ate made things worse. Carbohydrates brought agony.

When my oldest brother was diagnosed, at eighteen years old, with diabetes, I remember thinking, "I could never go without sugar!" Today, my diet is more restricted than his. I live on meat, eggs, and vegetables. I struggle to keep weight on, my gut remains tender, and I have to ration my energy. People express envy for my svelte body, but I tell them they wouldn't want to pay what I pay for it!

Despite all kinds of scans, tests, cleanses, antibiotics, antiparasitics, and visits to Stanford Medical Center and countless doctors, no one has identified or remedied the problem. If I eat carbs (this is the trigger, *not* stress, *not* guilt), the pain can increase to torture. I've lost track of the money spent on doctors and medicine, but I know which foods bring torment, and I'm satisfied the cause is purely physiological and not psychological.

Unsure I could continue an independent life for long, I returned to Utah to be closer to family (most live here now). It was a blessing. Not long after my arrival, my appendix burst, and I had family around me after emergency surgery.

I built myself a vibrant life in Utah. I had several books published, got engaged to a woman (though we later broke it off), got a master's degree, and began teaching college media courses. At the same time, I suffered increasing anxiety because I no longer had confidence in my ability to control my body. My professional and social lives were impacted by the fear of what might come out of my body at inopportune moments. I was dating, but each date was first stressful, then, eventually, a major effort (and sometimes humiliating). Soon, I would return from short dates completely exhausted.

It can be difficult to be sick and appear healthy. People in hospital beds don't get the same judgments as those of us who only appear well; I may be on my feet and participating, but I can't do everything a healthy person can. Sometimes I feel judged or misunderstood. All the same, despite discomfort and my ignorance of a remedy, so far, I've had the energy to do the essential things.

I had to alter my work to something I could do at home. Since I had been freelancing and had some books out, publishing became my focus. I was happy to find success, but it was lonely. My family and a couple of married friends became my only social contacts; they're wonderful and I love them, but that level of human contact wasn't enough.

Isolation is the worst thing for an addict, but it's pretty bad for just about anyone; neediness can ambush you in random casual human interactions.[1]

IT'S "NOT GOOD" TO BE ALONE

The move to Utah also brought me closer to certain judgments and the opportunity to come to terms with them. A few years ago, I learned that the brother just older than me has disapproved of me for some time. Though he considers himself an ally of LGBTQIA people, he doesn't feel his bi younger brother can offer him any insights on the topic.

It was particularly devastating to feel misunderstood by someone who has heard firsthand the messy details of my activities with men—yet who, apparently, doesn't know me. For years, I've sought peace with God and those around me, and I've learned much. Despite my openness about my past and my experiences, this brother dismisses, judges, and denounces me (mostly since cleaning up my act at age 28). Being misjudged is painful; being wrongly condemned by someone who should know me well and has professed love is worse.[2]

I no longer feel affirmed at some family gatherings. Even when I'm present in body, I'm guarded, and it can be lonely. While dejected, my attitude is that I must forgive. I anticipate enjoying all of my family when they love again. Some growth may only come in the next life.

My poor health and faltering family support increased my isolation. I even stopped dating and shelved the hope of a wife and family. Still, all these difficulties combined gave me time to rest and evaluate my relationships. Without these "setbacks," I would never have embarked on the discovery I'm writing about. I never dreamed relationships could be so rewarding until I'd lost poor ones that I'd clung to.

Perhaps you feel, as I did, that you could never live without carbs (or whatever you most delight in). I'm here to say that some of our most poignant losses often lead to gains far beyond what we so treasured before. What we see as our most painful difficulties can become our greatest opportunities.[3]

In 2018, I felt the need to expand my social circle in a new way. For me, tragedy brought me to the best chapter of my life.

POINTS TO PONDER

- Transitory euphoria cannot fulfill true needs (the self is never satisfied). What have you found that meets your real needs?

- Isolation is bad for just about anyone and worse for those of us trying to change behavior or overcome addiction. What tools and resources can you turn to when you feel isolated?

- Making sincere efforts to progress doesn't necessarily shield you from judgment and misunderstandings, even from those you want most to understand you. How can you establish a social circle that supports you through troubles or helps you avoid overreliance on the same person/s perpetually?

NOTES

1. Bible, Gen. 2:18.
2. "Many people today . . . are either unable to see things as they truly are or are unsatisfied with the truth. Moreover, there are forces at play today designed to deliberately lead us away from absolute truth. These deceptions and lies . . . often have dire, not minor, consequences." Gary E. Stevenson, "Deceive Me Not," *Ensign*, October 2019, https://www.churchofjesuschrist.org/study/general-conference/2019/10/45stevenson?lang=eng.
3. Ever know an athlete who, due to an injury, ended up in their ideal career?

CHAPTER 8

The Best News—How to Create Deep Same-Sex Connection

"We crave to be touched, looked at, admired, smiled at—to laugh with and feel safe."[1]

—*Counselor Marshall Burtcher*

I HAVE A STARTLING SECRET TO SHARE with you: You don't have to battle your libido, you don't have to repress it, and you don't have to surrender to your sex drive as the ruler of your life—it's *not* your enemy. Your libido can work for you as a helpful, though rudimentary, gauge that lets you know when you're neglecting human relating needs. Here's a roundabout explanation:

I postulate that sex is a thief to the deepest and most durable same-sex connection. Lots of people (including my past self) get sexual primarily because they know of no other way to connect with those of their own sex. It is amazing how many people have gone through life—as I did for years—believing there are only two ways to experience same-sex attraction: try to enjoy sex with someone of my sex or attempt to give up same-sex emotional needs entirely. For many years, I sought fulfillment in same-sex sexual relating, and while I experienced physical gratification, I never found the deep connection I yearned for. Rejecting that approach, I tried being a recluse. I also tried to marry the opposite sex, a solution which carries the possibility of giving up real same-sex emotional needs. All of these approaches left me hollow and discouraged, but I came to believe there had to be other options out there.

I was looking for something fulfilling that creates deep bonds, that acknowledges the nuances of my same-sex needs and lets me be informed by my libido rather than denying it or giving in to its immediate clamoring. There is an option that fills me better than any of those first either/or choices. It is deep, lasting union—and can be found in more ways than I describe here. I encourage you to find connection that meets your legitimate needs.[2]

MEETING LEGITIMATE SAME-SEX EMOTIONAL NEEDS

After ten years of isolation, I felt an impetus to be social again. (I hadn't been a total hermit, but contacts with just a few family members and friends were insufficient.) While I'm sure I'd had at least a passing awareness of it before, I was now quite aware of how much I had lacked for human touch. I had begun to feel resentment when greeting people: I would think, "That's a polite handshake, but an embrace would be better." My body and brain were signaling to me that I had an unmet need for physical connection and that it wasn't necessarily a sexual one.

I realized I had to accept people where they were with what they were willing to give; I also intuited that somewhere out there were people whose desire for emotional connection and affection was as great as mine, regardless of their sexual orientation. I started searching for platonic and asexual social sites. They were not easy to find. Eventually, I found a couple of them, though their few members were scattered around the globe.[3]

While I feared I might revert to compulsive sexual activity, I felt almost lead in this new direction. Though many sites declared themselves "nonsexual," each person I met still had to be vetted as to their true motivations. I eventually found a couple of local people who agreed to respect my boundaries.

Not everyone believed that all I wanted was to talk and embrace, and nothing sexual. But articulating my boundaries and sticking to them went a long way in making me credible and having people honor my objectives.

My first acquaintance in my nonsexual connection experiment had come from out of town and was staying in a hotel. I made him wait twenty-four hours after agreeing to meet! I wasn't sure that he, like me, only wanted emotional connection and affection. I wasn't sure how I'd do, either; I was concerned that I'd revert to old habits and violate the boundaries each of us had set. It had been years since I'd been sexual, and I didn't want to return to that insatiable lifestyle. When I met Tony at his hotel room, I asked to prop the door to the room wide open, and we remained clothed.

What happened next had never happened to me in all my previous (sexual) experiences—but it's a regular and constant part of my life now. No sooner did I realize that Tony wasn't after sex (I already knew I wasn't) than we opened up and bonded *profoundly*. The conversation was natural, and the connection and physical affection were so pleasant, it all seemed almost otherworldly.

I had felt deep yearning and passion for guys in my past. I believe I had initiated bonding with some men, but it always seemed to evaporate. Now, I know that dissipation happened after we got sexual—which was typically the pattern back then. This time, my "neediness" wasn't the priority, and it never became so. What I experienced was a near-total feeling of love and concern for Tony and a desire that he feel completely loved and accepted. I still feel that for him to this day. Our first meeting was in 2018, and though Tony's from the Midwest, he visits Utah regularly.

Searching my memory more deeply, I remembered I *had* experienced such bonding, years before. When I was a young man, I had a buddy who was very nurturing and affectionate but with whom I was never sexual. He and I had shared this same kind of bond, though I hadn't understood it for what it was at the time.

NEVER IN A MILLION YEARS

Same-sex connection isn't about finding a soul mate—though I'm not saying that couldn't happen—nor is it about playing around or using a person. It's about making my relationships as lasting and mutually rewarding as possible. Male love isn't a zero-sum thing (more on this in the next chapter).

Embracing a person nonsexually offers emotional and spiritual nourishment and can result in feelings of contentment and peace. Done right, holding and being held leaves a person feeling fulfilled—rather than hungry for sex. As long as the embrace is not sexualized, it can establish lasting emotional connectedness and deep intimacy without clinginess or dependence; compare this to a burst of sexual euphoria followed by a gradual or immediate drop in connectedness.[4]

Because the connection is with my gender, it is unique compared to other pairings or groupings. It's not sexual; its nature is deeper than friendship, beyond platonic, yet it's not spousal or other-halved. Significantly, it's not necessarily exclusive (though one-on-one *at a time* is best). It's the affirming exchanges that please independent of sexual relating. It establishes a genuine bond. If you reevaluate your relationships and previous expectations in light of the fulfilling nature of these unique connections, you may note that possessiveness and jealousy fade from the picture (see chapter 9).

In US culture, it's easy to miss beneficial experiences that satisfy our emotional appetites. So many of us—especially men!—are starving. More than one man has said to me that he'd never before experienced the depth of love felt while receiving safe affection from someone who understood his needs and wasn't trying to be sexual. Many men experience the exact epiphany that I did in holding—declaring to me, "*This* is what I've always wanted, but I never realized it until now!" (I suspect that many of us as youth were indeed aware of this true desire early on, but it was quickly eclipsed by the euphoria and distraction of sex.)

Heterosexual people also need same-sex connection, regardless of whether it involves physical affection. At a Sexaholics Anonymous (twelve-step) meeting, I met a man who struggled with pornography and lust for women. L.J. seemed tough, almost stern; I approached him with the hope of expanding my social circle (he, obviously, knew of my past compulsions with men). Not long after becoming friends, I explained to him my quest for nonsexual contact. L.J. shook his head and essentially said, "Never in a million years will that happen between you and me."

A couple months later, L.J. and I were sitting in his garage (I'd helped him move something there), and he put his arm around me. I put mine around him—then he wept. The surprise of contact with this resolutely heterosexual man was eclipsed by my utter astonishment at his reaction (though I just sat with him, hoping not to show surprise). I learned that day that just about anyone can experience deep need for affection from those of their sex. In fact, week after week, L.J. would invite me over, and we would sit and talk with arms around each other (sometimes with his wife chatting with us). I've since held other heterosexual men. All humans need connection and touch.

BOUNDARIES: TRUE CONNECTION'S PARADOX

Before any holding happens, all boundaries and desired outcomes should be articulated clearly by both people (recall that emotional need can manifest as sexual desire). Forgive my bluntness, but one of the best ways people understand that I am serious about not wanting to be sexual is to stay clothed. Touching skin can be healthful, but not wearing any clothing can easily be misinterpreted; one or both partners are susceptible to being sidetracked sexually. Even if one feels completely confident that they won't get sexual, that doesn't address the *other* person's feelings of vulnerability—not to mention what proximity and nakedness combined might trigger in either person's mind.[5]

It's inappropriate and defeats the purpose of holding to be in a situation where even one person is uncomfortable. Naked holding can be the result of social pressure, which is totally incongruent with the objectives of holding (and certainly with those of sex): Consent, not coercion, is at the root of all healthful and respectful interactions.[6] If you are sincere about nonsexual holding, don't propose or agree to combine it with nudity. Comfortable pants or shorts and a T-shirt can provide a helpful boundary.

Having more than one holding partner can help avoid too much reliance on any one person. Still, keep it to one partner at a time; my experience is that true connection is quite unlikely with more than two people present.

Both parties should articulate their needs and desires and decide together how holding might look for them (sitting side by side or in other positions). Make it understood that neither person will grab or rub against the groin or other sensitive areas of the other person or attempt to sexually arouse themselves or the other person.

Holding in silence for a time is fine, but if there is never conversation, a person might begin to fixate on bodies. Discover each other's stories, what each is learning or experiencing; laugh together. The objective here is emotional connection, and touch can be a means to that (if it doesn't supplant the ultimate goal of one-on-one affirmation).[7]

Even while holding, flexibility and rigidity have their place. Just because connecting was done one way doesn't mean it has to continue that way. You may discover that some things don't work or would be better than what has been articulated; speak your mind. Feel free to remind a person of your boundaries; you may need to physically move—or move part of their body—to maintain boundaries. Open communication is vital. Never assume that any individual is impervious to lust. Always speak up if something is not comfortable for you, and never rely on another person to maintain your boundaries; that is always your responsibility.[8] A caveat: While it is essential for you to keep your own boundaries, this should never have to be a battle. Your cuddle partner must understand and support your limits. If your holding companion has a problem with changes or with respecting boundaries, you may need to find someone else.[9]

Physical arousal is not uncommon; it's a normal biological reaction and doesn't necessarily mean that sex is on the agenda. It can be affirming to feel that someone is attractive or attracted; acknowledge it and continue your conversation. If arousal persists (and it might on many occasions), it may be best if that part of the body is not in contact with the partner until calmer.[10]

If we're honest about human nature, some guys say they want to "cuddle" as a way to get sexual, so when I don't get sexual, some express disappointment, even anger. Vetting potential holding partners and sincere disclosure are important safeguards to avoiding problems. Sometimes you can tell with the first chat or photo whether a person is sincere about not being sexual with you.

This discussion of boundaries for avoiding sexual relating brings us back to our friend, the libido. Historically, your default indicator of legitimate same-sex needs may be your libido. The libido (even an erection or other physical signs of arousal) isn't a precise barometer of what exactly is going on inside you, of what really needs attention. I've found that my libido is ninety-five percent an emotional indicator, a rudimentary "check engine" light for multiple subtle social needs. These are core needs that we may have little experience identifying, let alone successfully meeting.[11]

If you respond to an insistent libido at face value, your focus will be on yourself and your desires—and the self is never satisfied in self-seeking. Sex isn't a need; sexual attempts to satisfy a demanding sex drive only make it more demanding, making you a servant to your body's urges for ever more euphoric hits.

Real connection isn't about self but about relating with others. The next time your libido hollers for attention, rather than surrender to its in-your-face demands, ask yourself, "What's going on in my social world? Am I meeting my needs healthfully?"

If you're regularly meeting your emotional needs, you won't feel at war with your body—and you won't have to bottle up your feelings. The libido becomes very calm when emotional needs are met. Yes, I get erections—but I don't struggle with yearning; I bask in the affirming love that is filling me so overflowingly that I don't want for *anything* when embraces end (okay, perhaps a chocolate milkshake). This fulfillment lasts for days.

Intimacy can involve the senses and yet not be sexual. I find conversation, touch, emotional connection, and eye contact to be far greater and lasting than anything male-on-male sex offers. Is there thrill—even euphoria—in nonsexual holding? There is! Try it and observe how much better the relationship goes beyond touch.

If your libido is in the driver's seat rather than part of the instrument panel, or if you're steeped in delusions that same-sex sex is the best kind of connection or that the person you're with really wants sex even when they've said they don't, you're missing the point of human connection—and missing out on the most indelible union.

But what if you find yourself at the other end of the spectrum, craving connection but uncomfortable with physical touch or holding? There are a number of options in this chapter that don't involve touch but that build connection and intimacy. Affirming conversation is a super way to meet legitimate emotional needs—even without holding. Any work or leisure activity can be a bonding experience.

C. S. Lewis said nonsexual ties are "as great a love as Eros. . . . Few value it because few experience it. And the possibility of going through life without the experience is rooted in the fact which separates [it] so sharply from . . . other loves. . . . [Familial] affection and [Romantic] Eros were too obviously connected with our nerves. . . . But in . . . that luminous, tranquil, rational world of relationships freely *chosen*—you got away from all that. This alone, of all the loves, seemed to raise you to the level of gods or angels."[12]

THREE KEYS

Some people say, "I've cuddled with my partner—but sex is better." However, they are speaking of sexual euphoria, which never lasts; the profound connection I'm talking about only comes with restraint—but not perpetually, because when true needs are met, urges are calmed. To understand its value, true union has to be experienced and might require not being sexual with anyone of one's sex.

Until you bond nonsexually, connection will not yield its best rewards. If you are easily distracted by visual stimuli or the quest for orgasm, it may take you longer to connect and come to value three keys to lasting same-sex fulfillment:

A. A personal understanding that your attraction to those of your own sex is legitimate (though a person might not presently understand the best way to express it; see chapter 3)

B. A personal belief that the most satisfying, longest-lasting same-sex bonding happens nonsexually and that orgasms with those of one's own sex are nowhere near as deep or lasting a bond (this is commonly grasped in the first embrace with no sexual agenda; *many* people experience this initially, then— thinking more is more—obliterate it via sex)

C. A personal realization that—good as they are— orgasms and sexual relating with those of one's own sex, regardless of deep emotion, stunt deep lasting union

Don't battle your libido; assuage it. Ideally, you will experience emotional fulfillment early and become certain of the other ideas soon thereafter. While I experienced profound connection in my first holding session, you might not. Perhaps you connect best via different activities or simple conversation. Consider that old ways of thinking or relating might be holding you back; then, allow yourself to let go of relating options that don't serve you. The more you *personally* comprehend—via experiencing superior satisfaction—that nonsexual connection is deeper and more lasing than same-sex sex (and that same-sex sex detracts from connection), the more you will treasure other kinds of relating over sexual activities with those of your sex. If you can't get to a place where you believe at least two of the above keys—if you keep same-sex sex as "plan B"—you might never attain lasting same-sex fulfillment.

> *"When we say no to something, we say yes to something else."*[13]
> —Ganel-Lyn Condie

It's not just your actions but also what's on your mind. Indulging in same-sex sexual thoughts or acts increases their hold on a person and diminishes the unique and profound union few know can exist. This happens because these individuals' focus on sex prevents the growth that leads to resilient connection.

It's a mistake to think sexual thoughts are harmless. They might be common, but untamed, they can be frustrating and counterproductive to lasting satisfaction. This may sound obvious (or perhaps impossible to some, at first), but try to avoid sexual thoughts and fantasies—even when not with your activity/conversation/holding partner.

Don't try to simply manage these thoughts; I don't think I know a mortal capable of maintaining sexual thoughts or longing at a certain threshold. Surrender them entirely to a higher power or to an accountability partner. This *is* doable, though it may take practice.

Be honest with yourself. Maybe your thoughts are: "I think I want sex with this person, but I have a better, more durable outcome in mind." Desiring every good thing for your pal also reduces selfish urges—the best remedy is feeling pure love and your own fulfillment. Deep lasting connection takes more intention, but it yields superior rewards. Again, when my relationships fill the cup of my emotional need, sexual yearning is scarce; I feel more grounded and content overall.[14]

One surprising area of strength for me has come thanks to my addiction. Gay men in Utah are accustomed to arguing with people about church chastity standards (no extramarital, nonmonogamous, or same-sex sex; see opening questions in chapter 1). Once people learn that my relationships today are more satisfying than past sexual ones, their standard arguments about repressive religion evaporate.[15]

Some still pressure me to be sexual "as long as there is no penetration," as though this arbitrary delineation of what constitutes sex doesn't alter the nature and outcome of the interaction. For me, penis stimulation takes my focus off my holding partner and onto myself; it *never* meets my same-sex emotional needs.

Again, wanting more always leads to wanting more.

Sometimes I have to explain the hollowness and trauma of living under compulsion and being out of control; I rarely get pressured for sex after that. The part that some people are slow to contemplate is that I genuinely feel a greater connection in nurturing interactions than I ever did when seeking to satisfy physical urges. My male relationships today surpass previous ones, but not in spite of abstinence; they are superior *because* they are not sexual. I cannot describe the complete contentment of loving and being loved by someone who loves me for who I am, who isn't using me in an attempt to pacify emotional needs via sex.

You may balk at this, but judge it on your own: In sexual relations with those of your sex, how much is the other person's whole being your *primary* concern? In nonsexual connecting, I usually bond because I feel genuine care and love—I want every good thing for the person I'm with.

In the first embrace with my asexual but affectionate friend Stan, he and I each experienced mind-expanding epiphanies. Halfway through our cuddle and conversation, I realized that Stan had made zero efforts to push my boundaries. Some guys, excited by the novelty of contact or curious whether I'm serious about boundaries, "accidentally" brush a hand on my groin or subtly grind their pelvis into me to see how or whether I'll respond. Stan hadn't attempted anything of the sort. It was then that I realized that asexuality is real.

About the same time, Stan happily realized, "Karl's not trying to have sex with me!" He told me that he had connected with approximately two hundred men, each proclaiming they only wanted to cuddle; I was the first whose actions backed up my words. I've since cuddled with other homoromantic asexual people (some have more rigid boundaries than mine); we all have similar needs.

As you realize your true needs are being met, bliss and generous feelings toward others can replace self-absorption, even addiction. When someone feels fulfilled, images, fantasies, and even sexual propositions lose their allure. I no longer have to call a war council against lust. I cherish the deeper union I never found in the extremes of pretended independence or in detaching stimulation.

Nonsexual relating seems to be the ideal way for any two men or two women to meet true same-sex emotional needs. It's a paradox, but had I not found these bonds, my suppressed needs would likely have pulled me "off the wagon" again, in spite of—or due to—my previous isolating rules.

While I believe nonsexual same-sex relating is more profound than the average person experiences, some don't want the kind of interaction I describe, because not everyone is ready or willing to be vulnerable in this way—and not everyone experiences love via touch.[16] The me of thirty years ago might not have been able to stop at nonsexual holding (though I might have with a selfless guide). The me of even fifteen years ago would have run, afraid of my self.

This is what works for me, but it's just one way. I *don't* encourage it for minors or for any two people who lack experience controlling their passions. Likewise, if you are a sex addict or a people pleaser, you must be hypervigilant in maintaining personal boundaries in order to experience true whole-soul connection. An independent accountability partner that you check in with before or after connecting can help you avoid complications. Friends who speak the truth; who probe your choices, fuzzy logic, or rationalizations; and who remind you of your goals and commitments are priceless!

Remember how I wrote of frustration with my lack of progress early in my addiction? I later discovered I had legitimate need to connect with guys, that I couldn't ignore. Like my need for water, that need has never gone away (thank goodness).

You may have found a different way to meet your emotional needs—shared interests and activities, service, giving, or simple conversations where validation abounds.[17] Whatever you do, don't ignore real needs—isolation is poison. Spencer W. Kimball said that harm/offenses are "the result of deep and unmet needs."[18]

Regularly seek connection with others in healthful ways. Like oxygen, emotional fulfillment requires ongoing intake.[19] Tamping down or ignoring legitimate needs eventually fails. Long-suppressed needs find a way of expressing themselves, one way or another.

HAPPY HOMME, HAPPY HOME; HAPPY HER, HAPPY SIR

Reed, a gay friend who has been married to a woman for decades, concluded that sex with guys wouldn't fulfill him. He shared these ideas with his wife—and she whole-heartedly encouraged him to associate with me and other men who also feel that touch and emotional connection are true needs and that sex disrupts same-sex bonding.[20]

Guys, you need buddies! If you're married, it's an excellent idea to discuss your connection objectives with your spouse, including buddy-vetting criteria and how things will be kept nonsexual (chapter 9 details how this can become a person's preferred way to interact over some herculean act of resistance. A person whose needs are being met has little interest in same-sex sexual relating). Ultimately, every spouse must let their partner move about freely, because restricting a partner's access to others makes the marriage vulnerable to infidelity and other ills.

I've mostly discussed men, but clearly, women should keep girlfriends who share their goals and values—doing so meets a real need! If married, encourage your man to have wholesome male friends. You will both feel more well-rounded and socially and emotionally healthy, and you'll experience greater harmony when together.

Have a spouse or a same-sex partner you want to keep? These principles will do more toward keeping you together and eliminating jealousy than anything I know. They may even remedy cheating, not least because emotional needs are not confused with sex. Moreover, the relationship between you won't tend to fizzle like ones based on sexual euphoria; it's that pleasure basis which motivates a person to constantly seek sexual satisfaction elsewhere since euphoria doesn't last.

LIVING YOUR BEST LIFE

I genuinely believe that resilient same-sex bonding is very likely when people stop seeking same-sex orgasm as a means of satisfying emotional needs; I've experienced the difference. If your relationship has been damaged by selfishness or pleasure-seeking, know that same-sex bonds can be repaired. Bear in mind, though, that your most rewarding relationships may not be the one(s) you're in, pursuing, or longing for. A change in what you seek or how you seek it could save you decades of frustration and heartbreak and fulfill you beyond your current expectations.[21]

While avoiding heartbreak isn't the top priority, consider that looking at same-sex relationships from a different perspective can facilitate more enduring, healthful connections, which has the added benefit of reduced heartbreaks. If you're aware your libido is a legitimate (largely emotional) gauge, you can work with it rather than battling it, bottling it, or being its slave. Again, awareness of your options will empower you and increase satisfaction. Don't permit yourself to be driven by impulse—or to feel left out—for one more instant.

I'd bet you know a heterosexual man who, if honest, will tell you of a special bond he shares with another man or men that is both profound and unique to what he shares with his wife or girlfriend.

I present this not as a stopgap for people who wish to keep religious or other commitments—not as a way to *endure* temptation—but as a way to actually meet real needs and enjoy ongoing fulfillment.

"Over"-connecting won't fill you the way circumscribed emotional connection does.[22] In all my sexual activity (even in exclusive relationships), I never once experienced deep, lasting connection with a man until I tried it with no sexual agenda. Discipline truly yields the greatest payoffs.

POINTS TO PONDER

- To relate with those of one's sex in a lasting, fulfill-ing way, a person must gain their *own* conviction (not mine) of two or more of the following:
  A. Your attraction to those of your sex has legiti-mate purpose.
  B. Nonsexual same-sex connection fulfills best (leaving scarce room for lust, falling out of love).
  C. Same-sex sexual relations impede the deepest connection.

  You can work with your libido instead of battling it or being its slave. The libido becomes very calm when emotional needs are met. What have you observed about the ebb and flow of your own sex drive, and how is it affected by what's going on in the rest of your life?

- Same-sex sexual stimulation takes one's focus from the conversation/activity partner onto the self; it *never* meets same-sex emotional needs. The self is *never* satisfied. Naked holding or indulging in same-sex sexual thoughts also distract from true connection.

- Honest conversation is a super way to meet legitimate emotional needs—even without embracing. In your own experience, what ways of relating have been effective in building and nurturing emotional bonds?

- Physical arousal is a normal biological reaction in human relating; it doesn't necessarily mean sex is on the agenda.

- Male-female relations have their unique perks. Few people have experienced the particular fulfillment only achieved with those of one's own sex. What distinct joys and benefits do you notice in your varied relationships?

- Nonsexual same-sex connecting is *not* a technique to endure sexual yearning—it satisfies legitimate needs, reduces frustration, and brings joyful relationships that can last forever.

NOTES

1. Marshall Burtcher (personal social media post, 2022).

2. Addicts know that eliminating something from one's life requires that it be replaced (hopefully with something more beneficial). If you simply stop something and don't start something positive in its place, you're likely to go back to previous habits. (See, Bible, Matt. 12:43–45; Luke 11:24–26).

3. CuddleComfort.com (or search "ACE" or platonic groups. No site can guarantee that their members will behave in platonic ways).

4. See Vivian Manning-Schaffel, "The Health Benefits of Hugging," Better by Today, October 25, 2018, https://www.nbcnews.com/better/pop-culture/health-benefits-hugging-ncna920751; Ashley Uzer, "10 Health Benefits of Hugging, Backed by Science" MindBodyGreen, March 26, 2020, https://www.mindbodygreen.com/articles/hugging-health-benefits; Francis McGlone and Susannah Walker, "Four Ways Hugs Are Good for your Health," *Greater Good Magazine*, June 22, 2021, https://greatergood.berkeley.edu/article/item/four_ways_hugs_are_good_for_your_health; Erica Cirino, "What Are the Benefits of Hugging?" Healthline, last updated April 11, 2018, https://www.healthline.com/health/hugging-benefits#1.-Hugs-reduce-stress-by-showing-your-support.

5. Same-sex public nudity (bathing) was once common and can be healthful (generally, society has sexualized even this, so boundaries are needed here too). Yet, I believe nudity and cuddling do not go well *together* and should be separate activities. Russ Peterson, "Inoculating Children Against

Pornography" in *Faith in the Fire: An Outside Perspective on Latter-Day Families* (self-pub., Kindle Direct Publishing, 2021), Kindle.

6. See RiShawn Bittle, "How to Say No When It Counts," Full Focus, accessed August 21, 2022, https://fullfocus.co/say-no/.

7. Full body holding isn't necessarily unhealthy, but it can put one's focus on bodies rather than on soul connecting. Lingering on top of someone may be counterproductive in your goal to meet emotional needs and not be driven by physical urges. You'll need to understand yourself very well to be successful. If you desire to kiss, ask yourself: "Will kissing shift my focus away from healthfully meeting same-sex needs?" That's a personal question only you can answer.

8. While there might be natural consequences, you're not immoral for breaking a bad commitment.

9. Some boundary guidance: Chantelle Pattemore, "How to Set Boundaries in Your Relationships," Psych Central (blog), June 3, 2021, https://psychcentral.com/blog/why-healthy-relationships-always-have-boundaries-how-to-set-boundaries-in-yours.

10. Our focus often determines our reality. Please see endnote 7 in chapter 4.

11. See Marc DiJulio, "Male Sexuality and Emotional Needs," Innovative Men's Health (blog), n.d., https://innovativemen.com/blog/male-sexuality-and-emotional-needs; Wikipedia, s.v. "Sexual desire," last modified August 10, 2022, 10:24, https://en.wikipedia.org/wiki/Sexual_desire.

12. Lewis, *The Four Loves*, 92, 67, 58–59, 72–73, emphasis added.

13. Ganel-Lyn Condie, *You Are More Than Enough—You Are*

Magnificent (American Fork: Covenant Communications, 2018), 84. We would do well to forsake the "good" for the "better" or "best." Dallin H. Oaks, "Good, Better, Best," *Ensign*, November 2018, https://www.chur-chofjesuschrist.org/study/general-conference/2007/10/good-better-best?lang=eng.

14. A 24-hour technique addicts use that might enable a sex-focused person to attain appreciation for nonsexual connection is to say to sexual impulses, "Not today." "Lust only yields to the slow, patient working of the program" (or steps of surrender to God). *Sexaholics Anonymous* ("White Book"), 157. See also "Coming from AA, He Worked the Steps All Over Again in SA (Lawrence M., Virginia, USA)," Sexaholics Anonymous, n.d., https://www.sa.org/essay/coming-from-aa-he-worked-the-steps-all-over-again-in-sa-lawrence-m-virginia-usa/.

15. "Sharing becomes a liberating and life giving experience." *Sexaholics Anonymous,* 87.

16. Gary Chapman, *The 5 Love Languages: The Secret to Love that Lasts* (Winston-Salem: Northfield Publishing, 2014).

17. Chapman, *The 5 Love Languages.*

18. Kimball, *Ensign,* 1979.

19. Lewis, *The Four Loves,* 15

20. While my libido remains strong, my urges for sex are barely noticeable because my real needs are emotional. Since establishing especially deep and lasting connections, I almost never experience an impulse to self-stimulate (and it's never compelling).

21. The following are musts for any successful friendship or relationship: honesty, accountability, forgiveness, love, respect,

openness, loyalty, gentleness, acceptance, appreciation, trust, commitment, patience, recreation, sensitivity, and fascination. Of course, a person is most likely to find relationship happiness if they are already happy with self and with the world around them. See Karl W. Beckstrand, *The Joys of Male Connection* (Midvale, UT: Paths Press, November 2022).

CHAPTER 9

The Key to Lasting Same-Sex Relationships

I have had a rich life of brothers, men in my life that bless me in so many ways. Many of these brothers started out as a bromance. Meaning there was an attraction of some sort. Let's be real, attraction is one of the number one reasons we create friends in the first place. We are attracted to something about them. . . . I think bromances are healthy and wonderful. A bromance done right can . . . most often [turn] into a lifetime friendship.[1]

—Brad Petersen

AFTER THIS CHAPTER, I DON'T THINK you'll find it odd that I'm not into typical gay love stories and have no sexual designs on any man. (Again, please pardon the mostly male references; these are my experiences. I suspect much of what I say here also applies to women.)

My early relationships with men, like perhaps many of yours, didn't last long, even when we tried to make them last.

Knowing now how often sexual euphoria is confused with love and union, this doesn't surprise me. Today, I'm certain that, like the profound bonds some heterosexual men enjoy with each other, my current male (and female) relationships will continue to be close and rewarding forever.

As I began to enjoy deep, lasting connection with men, some guys inquired about becoming partners. It is understandable if a person's initial impulse in finding deep connection is to partner exclusively; the feelings of union can be solid and less likely to evaporate as they seem to when sexual climax is in the mix.

Exclusivity is fine, but sharing affection with multiple people may be more how your heart works toward those of your sex (and it has benefits). Remember that this type of bond does not presuppose the forsaking of other partners in the same way that marriage does. While I am not opposed to living with a like-minded man (someone who knows, as I do, that same-sex relationships are deepest and most durable when they are not sexual), I have encountered an unexpected dilemma: Some men wanting a live-together situation have wanted my heart *exclusively*, and I currently love *three* guys—deeply! My bonds with some men have endured for years.

ON JEALOUSY—A NEW MIND

You read that correctly: three. For a time, I felt like a freak among gay/bi men for loving more than one man. Then, a friend asked me whether I felt jealous when one of these three "soul brothers" spent time with—even held—another guy. My immediate and honest response was no.

I'd spoken that truth without thinking, so this was a mind-blowing revelation to *me*; it's what helped me grasp the secret of male relationships (though it shouldn't be a secret!—and it likely is the same among women). Not only are men capable of loving each other intensely and lastingly, if we don't try to fit into the male-female couple model, but also, there is no limit on how *many* soul brothers we can share profound love with—with no loss of love for anyone. And most men—straight or gay—are capable of great depth in most, if not all, of their same-sex relationships.

I wish I had a nickel for every gay husband who found himself attracted to a male guest at his own wedding. It's not because the newlywed is vile; he is simply a man—designed to love men (plural) deeply and uniquely from other kinds of love.

You may be content with having one "main squeeze"; just be aware of the nature of the male heart. Male love isn't a zero-sum thing (it's not a limited commodity that can run out). If you're ever drawn to a second man, it doesn't make you a reprobate, nor does it mean you love the first guy less; it may simply mean, unsurprisingly, that you're an ordinary man. You may already have found that you are capable of—or prone to—deep feelings for more than one guy. Honest heterosexual men will tell you this is normal. I'm persuaded that straight and gay women likewise feel deep love for multiple women in their lives.

You're not immoral for being drawn to more than one man—and you're not wicked if you have one guy who is special to you. You may be succeeding in pouring all of your guy love onto one partner. My perception of male love is that while that concentration *might* overwhelm an individual recipient, if there is overwhelm, it will most likely be within *you*. You may be bursting with feelings for other men, even ones you've just met (and perhaps beating yourself up over it). I suspect that love for people of our own sex is like fertilizer: most nurturing if spread broadly. Force it all into one spot, and you might kill the relationship.[2]

Again, having someone special is awesome; I *do* spend more time with one of my soul brothers than the others. He is happy to know that's the case, but he doesn't ask whether he's my favorite, and he doesn't worry when I spend time with someone else; this goes both ways. If your favorite guy isn't asking you for emotional exclusivity, don't take that chore upon yourself, even secretly (if he *is* asking it, you might consider carefully how healthful and doable such a request is for you).

Concentrating something that seems to be intended for broad distribution might incite needless jealousy, self-loathing, or discouragement. I don't discount special love between two people; remember too that same-sex bonds are different than opposite-sex bonds (I honestly feel they are deeper in many ways). If you're not sexual with your male circle, chances are that all such relations will be rewarding and lasting—you have discovered a key to long-term male love. How you interact with each person will, of course, vary (your feelings won't necessarily be equal for each guy).

Vern, a gay man in Salt Lake City, has had a boyfriend for many years. From what I understand, they are deeply committed to each other but are no longer sexual (by choice). This doesn't mean that they don't have social needs outside of their relationship. Vern sought my friendship as something safe because he felt that my lifestyle could never jeopardize his relationship with his boyfriend.

When we understand these deep bonds for what they are, neediness and jealousy fade. If you get a twinge of the green-eyed monster, as I thought I had a couple years ago, consider how much you might be being influenced by *romanticism*—the nonsensical dogma that persuades a person that a *true* love will know a person's unspoken thoughts and fulfill all needs or that sex equates to (or even trumps) unity. These ideas have harmed humanity in general for generations.[3] Overcoming our culture's harmful fixation on romance will help you to see your loved ones as they are and to love truly, deeply, and without jealousy. Indeed, C. S. Lewis described voluntary nonsexual relationships as "the least jealous of loves."[4]

If you examine your experiences with men, you may find, like I did, that what men sometimes mistake for a partner-type jealousy is actually a generalized human jealousy.[5] Think about it: Someone you love gives a hug to someone else; are you feeling hatred for the "competition" for taking up all your guy's love (impossible, because it isn't finite)—or do you wish the special guy showed you love in the same *way/degree* they show it to the other person? It doesn't mean your important guy doesn't love you! It may just be that they don't love you as deeply or spend as much time with you *as you wish*. This is a normal aspect of human relationships (people can be jealous of others' jobs, hobbies, or even religious practices because they take a special person's attention away).

My sense is that what some might refer to as emotional infidelity is impossible among people of the same sex. If we understand and accept that the male heart (heterosexual or gay) naturally tends toward deep love for multiple people of our sex, we won't worry much whether someone loves us as much or in the same way as they love someone else. We also won't have doubts about our own lack of commitment to a special guy when we experience emotional connections with other guys, and we won't feel possessive or afraid that our soul brother(s) might emotionally "cheat." We'll actually be okay with an intimate brother loving other men because we understand the natural workings of the human heart toward those of one's own sex.

Tad, a gay man who respects my boundaries, grasps that loving one man doesn't mean love can't exist with other men. While we share a deep closeness, neither of us feels possessive of the other, and each of us are close to other men.

If you see me with my arm around a guy, I'm not

signaling ownership or marking turf. The men in my life are not possessions; you are welcome to love them too. If you see me being affectionate with a guy, I hope it's an indicator that you can receive pure affection from me and, most importantly, that *you* can share healthful male affection with other men.

While I may tell a soul brother that I love him, each of us must comprehend that I am capable of feeling the same for other people simultaneously—and so is he![6] It is a gift to feel deep love for multiple people and recognize that it in no way diminishes the intensity of love that we two share. This depth, clarity, and freedom is directly connected to nonsexual relating.

It's liberating and healthful to discover the profound connection that's unique to people of the same sex, to understand that no eternal soul brother or soul sister relationship suffers for not conforming to the heterosexual couple model. Rather than compare the standards of chastity and fidelity in opposite-sex marriage to parameters for other kinds of relationships, it's simplest to recognize that heterosexual love and same-sex love are *not* competing loves; each is unique. There are infinite ways to love because there are multiple kinds of relationships and people!

Here's the best news of all, especially to those who've seen a lack of fidelity among men who are sexual with men: Because the general nature of male love isn't exclusive—and if you keep from mentally associating love with sexual euphoria—you're much less likely to fall out of "love" with a man you now love, even if you acknowledge love for another man.[7] Without this insight—that is, while seeking pleasure (or evading heartbreak)—a person is more likely to abandon one man after another. It's like gorging on empty calories and remaining hungry rather than feasting on the nourishment of same-sex emotional bonding.

I'm *not* preaching gay polyamory, because I'm not endorsing gay sex, much less with multiple partners. Yes, sexual euphoria is exhilarating, but nonsexual connection is *more* fulfilling and resilient (yet still euphoric)! Love and sex do not always go well together. Unfortunately, some have seen their love damaged or destroyed when sexual appetite overpowers consideration of another's comfort or consent. Such selfishness runs counter to true connection, and sex in these circumstances not only fails to meet legitimate emotional needs of the soul but also might deepen the yearning. By neglecting true emotional connection, the feeling of neediness persists, regardless of how much sex one has.[8]

My friend Lucas summed it up: "Once the high of wanting someone so intensely is recognized—not as love, but as euphoria inside the self—one can look toward the *other* man's happiness. And that joint happiness doesn't seem to involve orgasms." In other words, it's focusing on someone else's happiness that really feeds us. "'We all think we want to be loved, but what actually feels good to us is feeling loving,' clinical psychologist Lisa Firestone, Ph.D., tells *The Huffington Post*. . . . 'When we have feelings of caring or love for other people, we feel better.'"[9]

Love is a verb; it is a focus of attention on the other rather than the self. It involves seeing people as they are. True love involves giving of self with no thought of receiving. When we can do this, we will burst into a new level of consciousness, relating, and joy—and these things can be shared epiphanies beyond what we've previously experienced.

It can be difficult to grasp and accept this ideal of love, especially if you've been living with a different set of assumptions for a long time. As we're patient with ourselves and each other, we can see this selfless love have a positive impact in our lives.

John is a dear friend of multiple years who lives with a boyfriend who is not affectionate. They rarely have sex anymore. John really appreciates that I express love via touch, but he would often ask me for sex. I explained that the reason he and I are so close is *because* we're not sexual. One day, John stormed out of my place—determined not to return. "You're not giving me what I want," he said. "I guess I'll have to find it elsewhere."

Two or three days later, John came back. "I miss the emotion we share," he said. The kind of union John and I have isn't found in male-on-male sex. Still, he struggled to let go of the belief that mutual sexual ecstasy with me would only make our connection better. He fantasized about it and would occasionally masturbate when visiting me, when I wasn't in the room with him. After some weeks, he stopped. When we talked about it, he said our connection was better and longer lasting when he didn't masturbate. On days when he had masturbated, he soon wanted to leave; now, when he's here, he's reluctant to leave. He discovered this all on his own, and our friendship is better for it. I am not jealous of John's boyfriend, and John is not jealous of the other friends I share affection with.

When I contrast my past sexual relationships with the profound and lasting intimacy I now enjoy, there is simply no comparison. Far from practicing a grudging, hair-shirt celibacy, I gladly abstain from sex because I refuse to sacrifice my deep, affectionate bonds to return to meager same-sex sex.[10]

If I seem unromantic to you because I'm not drawn to gay love stories, understand it's because most fail to do justice to limitless and profound same-sex love—and because they seem deceptive regarding the resiliency of most sexual same-sex partnerships (also because my life is filled with real, *lasting* relationships).

POINTS TO PONDER

- Most people prefer loving to being loved; it is a gift to feel deep love for others, including those of one's sex. I believe that truly loving relationships can continue forever. How have different types of love fulfilled you in different ways?
- Heterosexual love and same-sex love are *not*

competing loves; each is unique, and all people are designed to love those of their own sex richly.

- Because nonsexual same-sex love isn't necessarily exclusive—and helps us not confuse love with sexual euphoria—falling "out of love" isn't common. How are you liberated in knowing you can share deep same-sex bonds with more than one "soul brother" or "soul sister"?

- There is an inverse relationship between the selfish pursuit of sexual gratification and the ability to engage in genuine, fulfilling sex-same emotional connections, with the latter more consistently offering durable fulfillment than the former. Does my observation surprise you? How have you seen this interplay at work in your own life?

NOTES

1. Life Coach "Chef" Brad Petersen, Facebook, winter 2022, https://www.facebook.com/profile.php?id=754211589.

2. "Putting the weight of all our deepest hopes and longings on the person we 'love' will crush him or her with our expectations." Timothy Keller, Facebook, spring 2022, https://www.facebook.com/TimKellerNYC.

3. The School of Life, "How Romanticism Ruined Love," YouTube video, May 30, 2016, https://www.youtube.com/watch?v=jltM5qYn25w; Mark Manson, "A Brief History of Romantic Love and Why It Kind of Sucks," Mark Manson: Life Advice That Doesn't Suck (blog), n.d., https://mark-manson.net/romantic-love; and Mark Manson, "Romance

Is Like Alcohol," Mark Manson: Life Advice That Doesn't Suck (blog), n.d., https://markmanson.net/romance. See also Ty Mansfield (quoting Robert Millet on theological [and cultural] viruses), "Balancing the Tensions of Our Latter-day Saint and LGBTQ Conversations," *Deseret News*, October 21, 2021, https://www.deseret.com/opinion/2021/10/21/22717022/balancing-the-tensions-of-our-latter-day-saint-and-lgbtq-conversations-mormon-truth-love.

4. Nonsexual "love, free from instinct, free from all duties but those which love has freely assumed, almost wholly free from jealousy, and free without qualification from the need to be needed, is eminently spiritual. It. . . . is the sort of love one can imagine between angels. Have we found the natural love which is Love itself?" Lewis, *The Four Loves*, 61, 77.

5. Lewis, 57.

6. I have held women, heterosexual and gay men, asexuals, and a transgendered person—each has been satisfying in different ways.

7. Life coach Brad Petersen says boyfriends get jealous and possessive; brothers don't:

> Another falsehood is . . . I am told that my love has limits, "Only so much to go around." If I were looking for [a boyfriend] perhaps that might be true, but in the search for brothers I have learned this very important lesson: The human heart, my heart and your heart, has an unlimited capacity to love as many as deeply as we want. There are no limits to the amount of brothers one can love and enjoy. . . . The more I love the greater my heart expands. After all, we are created in God's image and Christ is our

example in all things. His love knew and knows no limits. It is limitless. We have the same gift as Christ has: To love as many as deeply as we want, in other words, why limit how [deeply/many] we love? . . . "I don't need a boyfriend, I need brothers that respect me and help me to be closer to Christ, my dearest brother. I need men that love deeply and are aware, in the process, we . . . have to come to understand and control our mortal bodies." Chef Brad, Facebook, winter 2022.

8. See Jett Stone, "Why Men Need to Prioritize, and Celebrate, Their Friendships," Psychology Today (blog), February 8, 2022, https://www.psychologytoday.com/us/blog/the-souls-men/202202/why-men-need-prioritize-and-celebrate-their-friendships.

9. Lindsay Holmes, "8 Ways to Tell if You're a Truly Compassionate Person," *Huffington Post*, last updated December 7, 2017, emphasis added, https://www.huffingtonpost.co.uk/entry/habits-of-compassionate-people_n_5522941.

10. "Love is what you've been through with somebody." James Thurber, James Thurber Quotes. BrainyQuote.com, BrainyMedia Inc, accessed August 17, 2022, https://www.brainyquote.com/quotes/james_thurber_106549.

Authentic Identity— The Key to Happiness

Sexuality may operate without Eros [love] or as part of Eros. . . . I make the distinction...to limit our inquiry and without any moral implications. I am not at all subscribing to the popular idea that it is the absence or presence of [love] which makes the sexual act "impure" or "pure," degraded or fine, lawful or unlawful. If all who lay together without being in the state of [love] were abominable, we all come of tainted stock. The times and places in which marriage depends on Eros are in a small minority. Most of our ancestors were married off in early youth to partners chosen by their parents on grounds that had nothing to do with [love]. . . . And they did [fine]. . . . Conversely, this [sexual] act, done under the influence of a soaring and iridescent [Romantic love] which reduces the role of the [mind] to a minor consideration, may yet be plain adultery, may involve breaking a wife's heart, deceiving a husband, betraying a friend, polluting hospitality and deserting your children. It has not pleased God that the distinction between a sin and a duty should turn on fine feelings. This act, like any other, is justified (or not) by far more prosaic and definable criteria; by the keeping or breaking of promises, by justice or injustice, by charity or selfishness."[1]

—C. S. Lewis

CONSIDER THE INCLINATION TO BASE OUR decision-making on our feelings or sensations: A "good" decision is, ostensibly, one that makes us feel good, or at least avoids feeling bad. However, some "negative" emotions come from within us and have a positive purpose: Fear can preserve life and protect us from harm; anger can help us preserve justice; grief can help us love better and be less selfish; guilt can help us be more careful with people's things and feelings or reconcile with God.[2] (Shame, typically ignored guilt or societal pressure, is destructive and should be rejected.)[3]

Before I continue, I want to emphasize my belief that attraction to one's own sex is a gift—and something I would not change. If this is not abundantly clear, please re-read chapters 1, 4, and 5.

Perhaps you have experienced what I have on occasion: acting "badly" yet not feeling bad at all. Something a counselor shared with me applies both to lack of remorse and to self-loathing: Feelings by themselves are not the best gauge of personal progress toward happiness and are an incomplete basis for choices. Regardless of current feelings, facts provide better data and should hold most of our attention.

Being attracted to someone of your sex is *not* something to feel badly about.[4] Have a crush on someone who is taken or who could never be your partner? That's a tough spot to be in, but it's not necessarily evil. While feelings can seem to have a will of their own, when coupled with facts, they can help us know what is best.[5]

> *"You can't shame or hate yourself into lasting change."* [6]
>
> —Scott Cone

Understanding the positive roles of "negative" emotions can allow us to embrace them for personal development. Combined with facts, these feelings become our constructive servants rather than tyrannical masters.

Maria Shanley says, "Authenticity is a highly specific, constantly changing state. You have to live it, be it, make mistakes, admit them, learn from them, and therein inspire others to find it within themselves." [7]

Seeing and accepting yourself as you really are is essential. Coming out of the closet can be freeing and can lift your hopes. Refusing to be ashamed of who you are or what you feel is a great step forward. I encourage you to love yourself for who you are right now. The danger is in believing that the idea of self-discipline for higher goals comes from culture or church or a condemning god or that *all* enticements are worth pursuing. Labeling rules/aspirations as burdensome and rejecting them all is simplistic and risky.[8]

There are many dangers in indulging every appetite. In the case of sexual activity with few restraints, it can be addictive. Just as I did, you may find yourself going where you don't want to go and doing things you don't want to do with people you don't want to be with, ultimately becoming who you don't want to be. What some call "freedom" to be "authentic" can quickly morph into actual slavery to lust.[9]

It's a paradox: The surest way to *reduce* options is to reject any and all constraints, leaving no option off-limits. Often, rather than the desired pleasure being our servant, *we* become controlled by the thing we focus on. Freedom and opportunity are increased by the application of laws and boundaries. (A person who can't acknowledge equal and opposite reactions in everything will likely struggle to understand this.)[10]

Some people would rather carry shame than acknowledge weakness—which we all have. Some would rather pretend they've done no wrong or that right and wrong, offense and harm are social constructs. Is that truly liberation, or is it bondage?[11]

I submit to you that it *is* a lie to pretend you're heterosexual if you're not. Like other lies, it can be harmful to others and to yourself. Living a lie can be remedied by embracing who you are *and* by embracing all that you can become.[12] Pretending that no one is being hurt by abandoned standards or by redefining "harm" doesn't change facts; the destructive outcomes are overwhelmingly visible.[13]

Clearly, I'm not saying people must remain in miserable relationships. There are active and reflective methods to improving your situation from where you stand right now. Seek to resolve your relationships, and if necessary, end them with prudence; don't cheat and pretend it's not wrong or harmful. Don't be surprised if problems follow you once you're divorced, single, or in a new relationship; remember that dissatisfaction isn't always caused by spouse or family or culture. Chapters 8 and 9 have options (things arguably better than bond-stunting sex) that can enable a married or single person to feel fulfilled, honor vows, and not abandon or traumatize family needlessly.

PERHAPS YOU DON'T NEED WHAT YOU THINK YOU NEED

Many people view chastity as a lot of "don'ts." Some believe it is about one enormous Do, or more specifically, See! See people "as they really are."[14]

Eleanor Cain Adams and Allisa White write that we should make, "a conscious choice to respect and regard others as divine beings. Simply believing we're respectful in our relationships isn't enough." [15]

On the path of recovery, celibacy and sobriety do not necessarily mean healthful or fulfilled. Celibacy might be considered chastity, but chastity is not celibacy (and celibacy does not mean a person is pure in thought or motivation).

Embracing the *world's* version of being one's true self often means selfishness and disconnection from true union. This need not be permanent, but it can be difficult to understand—and escape (perhaps less easy than breaking a sex addiction).

Real authenticity, then, is being true to the divine in all of us. It's *in*authentic to pretend you are just an organism with only impulse for motivation rather than a sentient being with the powerful ability to choose/act—typically without compulsion, internal or external—if we are introspective and humble.

Remember that my counselor told me it's normal for most people to have conflicting desires? (Examples: sleep versus stay up; help others versus please self.) The best example might be the nearly universal desire to occasionally be away from people—yet be connected and a part of humanity at the same time.

Happiness depends on making conscientious/generous choices (ultimately) because we are personally persuaded that that is best now and in the long-term (not because someone else says so). While sometimes difficult, healthful choices are the best way to keep your options open (perhaps limitless). But they don't tend to require giving up all connections—positive relationships with those of our own sex are essential to well-being (see other kinds of relationships on page 71).

It's a paradox, but the ultimate free expression of one's true self can only happen with discipline. Even so, "[Discipline] is not about doing things perfectly, it's about doing things intentionally."[16]

The exhilaration of knowing you're attracted to your own sex and that you're priceless is real. The idea that anything you do is healthful is not.

If you think you can't live without sex, try going without and see (most people will likely be without a sexual partner at some point in life). If you're not sure you want sex, hold off for today; sex that you don't really want blocks intimacy. The connection almost all of us crave is jeopardized by self-centered physicality that opens a person to negative outcomes. Conversely, by choosing selfless and sincere relating, you can create connections far deeper than sexual ones—now—as an LGBTQIA person. Why wait?

POINTS TO PONDER

- All emotions can enlighten us: Guilt helps us maintain relationships, freedom, and growth. Shame, by contrast, hinders growth and distances us from reality. How can you discern whether you're feeling guilt or shame?
- The surest way to reduce options is to reject constraints. Principles and boundaries can *increase* options (having or getting all you want can lead to bondage). How have you seen this paradox at work in your life?
- Because they're based on deprivation and denial, celibacy and sobriety don't necessarily mean healthful or whole (it's possible to be sexual and sober; a person can be celibate yet not sober). Chastity deepens love in *all* our relationships now and always.
- Are you ever surprised by your choices, and what do you learn when that happens?
- No mortal can meet all your needs. True intimacy can't be attained if one is out of sync with self or

with the universe. How do you find balance and centeredness?

NOTES

1. Lewis, *The Four Loves*, 92.
2. Russ Peterson, *The Technology of Survival* (not yet published).
3. See Wendy Ulrich, "3 Ways to Combat Shame and the Difference between Guilt and Shame and Why It Matters," *LDS Living*, December 27, 2018, https://www.ldsliving.com/3-ways-to-combat-shame-the-difference-between-guilt-and-shame-and-why-it-matters/s/89594.
4. See https://PremioBooks.com or final page QR code.
5. "Feelings . . . are part of our legitimate nature and serve a useful purpose. . . . We don't feel ashamed or guilty for feeling hungry!" "Fostering a Positive Perspective of Sexuality," *Ensign*, August 2020, 72, https://www.churchofjesuschrist.org/study/ensign/2020/08/young-adults/fostering-a-positive-perspective-of-sexuality?lang=eng. Neither the scriptures nor The Church of Jesus Christ of Latter-day Saints condemn loving emotions between people of the same-sex (it's a gift). See 1 Sam. 18:1–5, 20:16–17, 20:41–42, 23:16–18; 2 Sam. 1:26; John 13:23, 19:25–27. See also The Book of Mormon: Another Testament of Jesus Christ (Salt Lake City: The Church of Jesus Christ of Latter-day Saints, 1829/2013) Alma 53:2.
6. Scott Cone (personal social media post, 2022).
7. Maria Shanley, "Learning What Authenticity Means to You," LinkedIn Pulse, April 1, 2022, https://www.linkedin.com/pulse/what-authenticity-means-you-maria-marie-shanley/?trackingId=L14Kl5jfQuu5YE7wVHLiiQ%3D%3D.

8. Standards can help us avoid serious injury. Von Keetch traveled to a bay in Australia renowned for its surfing. He met some American surfers who were upset that a heavy mesh barrier had been stretched across the mouth of the bay, right where the best waves were breaking. According to the surfers, the barrier went all the way to the ocean floor, ruining their "once-in-a-lifetime" surfing trip. An older, local man had them each look through his binoculars. What they saw were the dorsal fins of large sharks feeding near the reef on the other side of the barrier. "The old surfer . . . said: 'Don't be too critical of the barrier. . . . It's the only thing that's keeping you from being devoured.' Our perspective . . . changed. A barrier that had seemed . . . to curtail the fun and excitement . . . had become . . . protection. . . . We often cannot comprehend the great dangers hidden . . . below the surface." Von G. Keetch, "Blessed and Happy Are Those Who Keep the Commandments of God," *Ensign*, October 2015, https://www.churchofjesuschrist.org/media/video/2016-09-0009-blessed-and-happy-are-those-who-keep-the-command-ments-of-god?lang=eng.

9. Please allow my experiences (and those you've observed around you) to serve in place of any you might not yet have, and let my cautionary example help you have increased options via positive choices.

10. See Helen Yu and Alison Guernsey, "What is the Rule of Law?" Freedom School, last updated February 22, 2022, https://freedom-school.com/law/what-is-the-rule-of-law.html.

11. How long can a relativist retain values if everything is equally valueless to them? I've seen trust and families crushed by people who claim they are simply being authentic or

honest. Yes, life inflicts enormous pressures, but can a person be satisfied with the response, "It was either them or me"? *That idea comes from limited either/or thinking.* See Dan Peterson, "Is Morality Merely an Illusion?" Sic et Non (blog), Patheos, August 14, 2022, https://www.patheos.com/blogs/danpeterson/2019/07/is-morality-merely-an-illusion.html?utm_medium=social&utm_source=share_bar#Yd-8jylqXChXQHPCB.01.

12. "Coming out" may be only with oneself (whom one is attracted to is not everyone's business). "A man who lies to himself, and believes his own lies becomes unable to recognize truth, either in himself or in anyone else, and he ends up losing respect for himself and for others. When he has no respect for anyone, he can no longer love, and, in order to divert himself, having no love in him, he yields to his impulses, indulges in the lowest forms of pleasure, and behaves in the end like an animal. And it all comes from lying—lying to others and to yourself." Fyodor Dostoevsky, AZQuotes, AZQuotes.com, 2022, accessed August 17, 2022, https://www.azquotes.com/quote/588022.

13. See Nicole Howell, "A Link Between Single Parent Families and Crime (PhD diss., Olivet Nazarene University, 2015), https://digitalcommons.olivet.edu/cgi/viewcontent.cgi?article=1078&context=edd_diss; Vanessa Hemovich and William D. Crano, "Family Structure and Adolescent Drug Use: An Exploration of Single-Parent Families," *Substance Use & Misuse* 44, no. 14 (December 14, 2009), https://doi.org/10.3109/10826080902858375; R. L. Maginnis, "Single-Parent Families Cause Juvenile Crime" in *Juvenile Crime: Opposing Viewpoints* (Farmington Hills, MI: Greenhaven

Press, 1997), 62–66, https://www.ojp.gov/ncjrs/virtu-al-library/abstracts/single-parent-families-cause-juve-nile-crime-juvenile-crime-opposing; Kay Hymowitz, "The Real, Complex Connection between Single-Parent Families and Crime," *The Atlantic*, December 3, 2012, https://www.theatlantic.com/sexes/archive/2012/12/the-real-complex-connection-between-single-parent-fam-ilies-and-crime/265860/; "Effects of Fatherless Families on Crime Rates," MARRIpedia, n.d., http://marripedia.org/effects_of_fatherless_families_on_crime_rates. For more information on societal disintegration via sexual license (individual and societal), see Kirk Durston, "Why Sexual Morality May Be Far More Important Than You Ever Thought," Thoughts About God, Truth, and Beauty (blog), n.d., https://www.kirkdurston.com/blog/unwin.

14. Book of Mormon, Jac. 4:13.

15. Eleanor Cain Adams and Allisa White, "Living the Law of Chastity in a Dating World Full of Gray Areas," *Ensign*, August 2020, https://www.churchofjesuschrist.org/study/ensign/2020/08/young-adults/living-the-law-of-chastity-in-a-dating-world-full-of-gray-areas?lang=eng. See also Emily Madsen Reynolds, "Virtue and Abundant Life," *BYU Magazine*, Summer 2011, 47, https://magazine-dev.byu.edu/article/virtue-abundant-life/ and Juli Slattery, *God, Sex, and Your Marriage* (Chicago: Moody Publishers, 2022).

16. Dieter F. Uchtdorf, "Your Great Adventure," *Ensign*, December 2019, https://www.churchofjesuschrist.org/study/general-conference/2019/10/43uchtdorf?lang=eng.

CHAPTER 11

How to Not Miss Out— Commitment & Joy

"Don't lose faith in yourself." [1]

—*Hank Smith*

POWERLESS—YET WITH MORE THAN TWO CHOICES IN MOST THINGS

WHAT IF YOUR CHALLENGE ISN'T IN acknowledging natural (or even moral) law? What if your challenge is feeling *incapable* of living it? As an addict, I know that feeling intimately; it can be completely disheartening![2]

Inadequacy is part of being human. We can convince ourselves that responsible life is too hard, so 'why try?'. It is okay to feel like you can't meet all your ideals (you can't!), yet they are still worth having, working toward.

Comparing ourselves to others who have strengths different from ours can be discouraging. Some who believe in God might feel that weakness makes them unwanted or unloved (not true). Other people might deny weakness and delude themselves into believing they are entirely self-sufficient (at least temporarily).

But there are actual benefits to weakness. Weakness can help us appreciate and sympathize with other people. It can also help us not be cocky or irritating to be around!

ALL HANDS

Due to a childhood accident, my mom's nervous system was a mess for most of her life. Her body often wouldn't do what her brain told it to do. She would have so much pain and pressure in her head, she would sometimes crumple in a heap of sobs. While growing up, I watched her seek the laying on of hands by church members repeatedly.

As a teen, I asked her why she bothered to seek such blessings when it was "obvious" they didn't cure her. Her answer was emphatic: "Those blessings are what get me through!"

I came to believe that my mother found value in her frailty. I am forever grateful for the lesson she taught me that, though I may not get a total change of this or that circumstance; I am stronger than I know—and hope enables me to tap that strength and get through, one day at a time (I also believe God grants us empowering grace, though imperceptible to distracted eyes). There are things we can learn—even from suffering.[3]

Perhaps happiness is totally counterintuitive; perhaps it comes from giving of self to bless others (not in a martyr/

self-destructive kind of way). Perhaps, the more we seek to gratify the self, the less pleasure we find in anything.

Opposition helps us learn who we truly are, what we really value, and what we are capable of. I've learned that my differences are a gift that help me cherish diversity (how much could we learn from clones of ourselves?) and—gradually—gain empathy for people in trials that I cannot comprehend. Working to understand myself and others has (over time) brought me profound insights and rewarding relationships.

Remember the secret I discovered when I committed to be chaste on my mission? When we commit sincerely, it doesn't mean we are capable of fulfilling the commitment, but I believe our determination unlocks power beyond our own. I've seen it in my own life.[4]

> "The moment one definitely commits oneself, then providence moves too."[5]
>
> – William H. Murray

"Impossible" scenarios may be the key to understanding and getting the most from mortality. Some beauty—perhaps the most beautiful views and experiences—can only be seen or appreciated in suffering. Some people's greatest abilities would never be discovered without struggle (also if there were no one to comfort or console or empathize with).[6]

POWERFUL WEAKNESS

I finally grasped through the gift of my addiction that I don't have the power to transform myself. Had I not been persuaded so completely of my impotence by the chains of compulsive behavior, I may never have truly looked outside of myself for victory over compulsion. This intensely honest acknowledgment of powerlessness unlocks previously unreachable power.[7]

Still, the changes I experienced were not the ones I'd expected! I once hoped to avoid every attractive man, limiting my interactions with them to the necessary work for my career and church. Instead, I've been able to improve how I interact with men and *increase* that interaction in healthful ways.

I GUESS I CONFESS

Recall how for years I did everything I could think of to be free of sexual compulsion—without success. No amount of willpower or prayer was freeing me. When I demonstrated sincerity by doing whatever I could think of to acknowledge my impotence against compulsions (in my case, speak with other people about all my feelings and deeds), I began to receive the power I lacked.

Typically, I felt most comfortable telling other men: a counselor, a bishop, my oldest brother, and twelve-step companions. Confession is an essential, powerful key to freedom. By not being rejected—by being loved in spite of past choices—I felt the new joy of acceptance by men that was not tied to sex. My needs began to be met; power over compulsion came via my declarations of powerlessness! (I acknowledge that not everyone gets a supportive response from people.)[8]

Honesty not only helps me retain free will, get back on track, and overcome compulsions; it also serves as a kind of insurance *before* a crisis. Confessing desires contrary to my higher goals to another person typically eases selfishness's in-the-moment intensity.

Honest openness will not remove all trials, and no amount of disclosure or self-denial will remove our legitimate need for healthful connection with others; but candor with self and others (including God) can connect us to power above and beyond our own and minimize compulsion.[9]

By meeting my legitimate need for male connection, and by being open and honest, I (with grace) gradually regained rational decision-making power over my social relating and my life. Because unmet needs were no longer constantly foremost in my mind, all of my human interactions improved. I'm evolving. I'm still bi in orientation, and I'm happy about that. Now, because I am surrounded by affectionate people, I don't go overboard trying to meet those needs for connection. My objective is relating rather than euphoria, though I do get both.

A caveat: While my experience with compulsion and later freedom indicate that anyone can overcome addiction (I'm in no way extraordinary), experimenting with potentially addictive things is dangerous, not because addiction can't be overcome, but because such things can overwhelm a person. In the thick of slavery to self, some people give up, thinking that they are beyond hope.[10]

Life is paradox. Perhaps some people are experiencing profound disappointment that life isn't unfolding as they anticipated. If this is you, you're not alone![6] While you may have issues with life's timing or methods, we cannot declare life to be bad—especially if good outcomes can result from even "bad" things. The fact that many desired outcomes take time and/or effort, only means that there is value in every day and in every life.

Some solutions/growth cannot come instantly. I believe some things are beyond our power, yet patient optimism is a power itself. I ache with anyone who sees only permanence in mortal circumstance and life's paradoxes. I lament any notion that would limit options and joys.

I still have temporal struggles. I'm still required to regularly and healthfully meet my same-sex emotional needs— but providence is placing amazing people in my path.[11]

Knowing one's self and honest accountability with others (while retaining hope) are powerful tools toward retaining free will and reaching higher goals. Keep these handy—you may surprise yourself with the results.

POINTS TO PONDER

- Opposition helps us learn who we are, what we really value, and what we are capable of. In what ways has opposition helped you know yourself better?

- "Impossible" scenarios, paradoxes, and differences provide us opportunities to stretch beyond our present capacities and develop empathy.

- Binding ourselves to personal standards or principles makes us the most free. Whereas "freeing" ourselves from rules or boundaries can enslave us to our own desires. How does this understanding affect the way you make decisions?

- Everyone has weakness. We can accept all trouble as permanent *or* find ways to grow beyond as many limitations as we can. How can recognizing your weakness strengthen you?

- The ultimate expression of true self can only happen with discipline. Still, discipline "is not about doing things perfectly, it's about doing things intentionally." How do intent and discipline help reveal your true self?

NOTES

1. Hank Smith, 2022, (Facebook, April 11, 2022), https://www.facebook.com/photo.php?fbid=559296005557989&set=pb.100044327834890.-2207520000..&type=3.

2. "You're not a hypocrite because you have a bad habit you are trying to break. You are a hypocrite if you hide it, lie

about it, or try to convince yourself [God] has the problem for maintaining such high standards. Being honest about your actions and taking steps to move forward is not being a hypocrite. . . . [Spend] . . . less time hating [self]." Bradley R. Wilcox, "Worthiness Is Not Flawlessness," *Liahona*, November 2021, 62.

3. A family story my mother used to tell about her great-grandmother demonstrates how rather than hoping to be problem-fee, we get through difficulty one day at a time. Karl Beckstrand, *Agnes's Rescue* (Midvale, UT: Premio Publishing, 2021).

4. Book of Mormon, Ether 12:27.

5. William H. Murray, LeanCX, December 1, 2020, http://www.leancxscore.com/leadership-quote-william-h-murray-on-commitment-and-providence/.

6. See What Helps Me to See Beauty Even When There is Suffering?, accessed September 21, 2022, https://gratefulness.org/question-for-the-day/what-helps-me-to-see-beauty-even-when-there-is-suffering/.

7. I'm finally realizing there are no totally negative experiences; even the worst circumstances teach me and make me wiser. How you live affects—for good or bad—your beliefs.

8. Clearly, there are people who show little tolerance (and sometimes hatred) for differences. (I believe this is a fear of the unknown and that if we knew how enriching differences can be, we'd regularly seek out people different from us—and love sharing with them.) See Appendix G (online: https://GayAdored.com) for more insights.

9. See Linda K. Burton, "The Power, Joy, and Love of Covenant Keeping," *Ensign*, November 2013, https://www.churchofjesuschrist.org/study/general-conference/2013/10/the-power-joy-and-love-of-covenant-keeping?lang=eng.

10. D. Todd Christofferson, "Free Forever, to Act for Themselves," *Ensign*, October 2014, https://www.churchofjesuschrist.org/study/general-conference/2014/10/free-forever-to-act-for-themselves?lang=eng. 10.   Dieter F. Uchtdorf, "A Yearning for Home," *Ensign*, November 2017, https://www.churchofjesuschrist.org/study/general-conference/2017/10/a-yearning-for-home?lang=eng.

11. See appendixes and https://GayAdored.com (or final page QR code) for practical insight on meeting needs and for more tools for regaining/retaining free will.

CHAPTER 12

Is Mixed-Orientation Marriage a Happy Option for Some Attracted to Their Own Sex?

> "Well, actually, I didn't choose who I fell in love with. It just happened. I am attracted to men, and [to my wife] Susan."[1]
>
> —Brett Croche

AS I'VE ALREADY SHARED, I SOUGHT marriage to different women multiple times for a number of positive reasons. When my relationships with women ended—breakups were about evenly split between me calling it off and the ladies doing so—it was rarely because of my attraction to men. I typically didn't share that aspect of my life unless we were seriously contemplating marriage. However, when I disclosed my orientation to the girl I most want-ed to marry, she dumped me—adding that she wouldn't recommend me to any woman. That was quite a blow. It's important to note that not all women responded this way when I shared this vital part of who I am.

Many people who are attracted to their own sex have never acted on those feelings. Some married someone of the opposite sex and had families; some wanted to, and others felt led to marriage by God. Those who argue that a mixed-orientation marriage (gay/bi man with a heterosex-ual woman or lesbian/bi woman with a heterosexual man) cheats the nongay spouse might not be acknowledging that person's agency and ability to reason, so long as the gay spouse disclosed their sexual orientation when contem-plating marriage. Importantly, some men found no women attractive *except* for the one they married.

Some in mixed-orientation marriages felt pressured to marry by family or by church leaders. Some naively believed that marriage would "resolve" or "cure" same-sex attraction; if anyone was counseled that this would be the outcome, that is grievous.

Though there's an unfortunate history of well-meaning but misguided clergy giving bad instruction in counseling their same-sex–attracted parishioners, today, no faith-fully informed spiritual or other leader counsels people to marry as a means of managing or eliminating same-sex attraction.[2]

Mixed-orientation marriages are complicated, but even those that end can bring blessings. Interestingly, the gay parents I know don't regret having had children in mixed-orientation marriages. On the contrary, they say their children (and other things) made marriage worth any effort or sacrifice—even if they later divorced. It's notable that these parents are quick to say that their children are the greatest blessing of their lives.

Many people in mixed-orientation marriages are content where they are, and I suspect these couples are vastly undercounted. They have weighed the pros and cons and have decided they prefer the cooperative roles and returns that "traditional" union offers. We don't hear about these couples much because they don't typically broadcast their status or their experiences. Some people argue that such people are in denial or are controlled by religion. The reality is that while some young adults might be in denial about personal attractions, most adults come to be pretty certain about feelings in that area and have based their relationships on deliberate decisions.

By contrast, some same-sex–attracted people are not content in mixed-orientation marriage and feel they are living a lie. Some become overwhelmed by the real and legitimate need to connect with those of their own sex in some way because that particular social and emotional need is not met by an opposite-sex spouse.

Whatever your past or current domestic situation, I hope that my experience may inform your journey toward fulfillment and spare you or someone you love worse pain than what you or they might currently know. I am *not* about to propose that you bottle up your feelings or deny your true self. There are happy options beyond the closet, potentially isolating marriages, or a sexualized gay scene.

Some married people secretly hook up sexually with people of their sex. Some declare their situation to their spouses and divorce; others declare their feelings and work to stay married. I have met a great many people in a variety of situations. Those who embrace gay sex believe that this new way of life is the honest, authentic way to be— free from obligations. Others begin a disciplined, but disappointing, quest for one person who will meet *all* their same-sex partner expectations.

Some seeking a same-sex partner are unpleasantly surprised to find that gays are imperfect too, full of the same flaws, vices, and annoying quirks an opposite-sex partner might have. In my experience—speaking generally—gay men are more fickle than the many strong and beautiful women I've known who incline toward fidelity. I believe there are fundamental reasons for this (and will address them shortly).

Even in functional mixed-orientation marriages, trust can be an ongoing issue. Some of my gay and bi guy friends who are married to women are in situations where, regardless of fidelity to their wives, they are required to account to their wives 24/7 as to their whereabouts. Heaven forbid any of them should be delayed! One friend in particular is afraid he won't have access to his grandchildren if his wife decides she doesn't want him around anymore, so he submits to her perpetual accounting of his whereabouts.

What if the shoe is on the other foot, and you're the opposite-sex spouse? Are you afraid your same-sex–attracted spouse might get sexual with a gay person? Are you willing to trust your spouse in close, emotionally bonded relationships with their same-sex friends? Do you encourage those relationships and the time spent on them? Sexual infidelity is more likely to happen when legitimate social and emotional needs *aren't* met healthfully.

Consider that no one person can meet all of another's needs, even among spouses. Your spouse's healthy same-sex relationships (and yours!) aren't likely to erode your marriage but strengthen it by adding to your individual wholeness. Consider that your spouse may be unable to find a heterosexual person who will share the weight of their unique struggles through talk, touch, and comfort; they might *only* find a gay same-sex friend willing to do that. Yes, there is a risk of sex, but it's comparable to the infidelity risk of a heterosexual marriage; has any spouse, in all of history, been free of the risk of being cheated on? Trusting our loved ones can significantly reduce anxiety and pain.[3]

While our greatest joys may come from relationships, long-term bliss with a *partner* is elusive. Straight or gay, true fulfillment may not look like what we currently imagine it to be.[7] Relationships between people of the same sex can be among the most profound and rewarding, but they often manifest distinctly from what the world tells us to expect.

Same-sex relationships can create bonds that can last forever if the participants are true to the unique expressions of such love. The simplistic partnering stories the world tells to and about gays can create agonizingly destructive expectations, though it's worth noting that "romanticism" creates impossible expectations for people of all orientations. All the same, there is more than hope for happy same-sex relationships for those willing to scrutinize and perhaps adjust what they currently believe leads to lasting fulfillment. I'm not speaking of learning to live with the next best thing—nor with sexual infidelity—but of a path to lasting fulfillment and intimacy.[4]

These are not "pray-away-the-gay" scenarios. I firmly believe individuals can add to and expand worthy desires (not that it's a mandate; but we are creatures of change/ growth in just about every way). Regardless of orientation, the core draw toward one's own sex isn't just legitimate—it is essential (so, it may be that the people in need of the most expansion are straight—though many have discovered and embraced this personal amplification).

POINTS TO PONDER

- Awareness of options empowers us and increases our chances for fulfillment. There are happier options than what the world highlights for us: the closet, potentially isolating marriages, or a sexual-ized gay scene—better choices for relating to one another. What might other options look like for you or your loved one(s)?

- Most LGBTQIA parents count their children among their greatest blessings. In what ways have you been blessed while still seeking your particular path?

- Same-sex relationships *can* involve profound bond-ing that can, with care, last forever. How can you find and maintain such relationships?

NOTES

1. Brett Croche (personal social media post, 2022).

2. "Marriage should not be viewed as a therapeutic step to solve [differences]." Gordon B. Hinckley, "Reverence and Morality," *Ensign*, May 1987, https://www.churchofje-suschrist.org/study/general-conference/1987/04/rever-ence-and-morality?lang=eng. See also Gospel Topics, "Same Sex Attraction," https://www.churchofjesuschrist.org/study/manual/gospel-topics/same-sex-attraction?lang=eng. Church of Jesus Christ leaders are typically unpaid.

3. Chapter 9 has more insights on why gay men are often pro-miscuous, generally speaking.

4. According to the CDC, the "percentage of marriages that end in divorce in the US varies between 40% and 50%," and that number is falling (yet, so is the marriage rate). "The Williams Institute at the UCLA School of Law did publish data which suggested that the same-sex divorce rate was approximately

half of the different-sex divorce rate. However, *this was later retracted due to an error* in the calculation of the data." Note that "as same-sex marriages were only recognized on a federal level in the USA in 2013, there is still a lack of data regarding the rate of same-sex divorces." Branka Vuleta, "Divorce Rate in America (35 Stunning Stats for 2022)," Legal Jobs (blog), January 28, 2021, emphasis added, https://legaljobs.io/blog/ divorce-rate-in-america/. Some studies show greater satisfaction in gay marriages (than heterosexual) but greater *longevity* in heterosexual marriages; causation will likely be debated long-term. Theresa E. DiDonato, "Are Same-Sex or Heterosexual Relationships More Stable?" Psychology Today (blog), October 11, 2017, https://www.psychol-ogytoday.com/us/blog/meet-catch-and-keep/201710/ are-same-sex-or-heterosexual-relationships-more-stable. See also Benjamin R. Karney and Thomas N. Bradbury, "Research on Marital Satisfaction and Stability in the 2010s: Challenging Conventional Wisdom," *Journal of Marriage and Family* 82, no. 1 (January 2020): 100–116, https://doi. org/10.1111/jomf.12635; Lois M. Cochran, "A Religious Upbringing May Reduce Divorce Risk—But Probably Not for the Reason You Think," *Deseret News*, December 18, 2021, https://tinyurl.com/ff6xxtb3.

CHAPTER 13

What's Good About Attraction to One's Own Sex?—Your Unique Path

To choose is our gift and our right. I hope to have opened many options to you. Not every option is of equal value. Choose well. Choose joy!

C AN OPPOSITION AND COMPETING DESIRES BE good things? I have seen time and again, in my life and in the lives of others, things that, on the surface, looked like tragedies become great blessings. This book highlights several such scenarios. More than likely, you have seen similar things in your life too.

Date, disillusionment, do it again, doesn't seem to lead to fulfillment among people of the same sex. It seems there needs to be some thought, boundaries, and objectives to the process in order to achieve what seems so elusive.

Have you ever read or watched a story of a mortal who is granted omnipotence? If it's a well-thought-out portrayal, it will show how overwhelming and potentially destructive such power can be to its undeveloped holder. I believe we have challenging differences throughout our lives to grow. By navigating the consequences of our own and others' choices, we learn increasing patience, compassion, self-mastery, and love for ourselves and others.[1] This all seems to me to be preparing us to (eventually?) achieve a higher state of consciousness (greater power from understanding the laws of physics/nature/the universe) without being overcome by it.[2]

I've heard addicts say they are grateful for addiction—as am I, for bringing me to honest humble acknowledgment that *I am not God* (thank goodness) and that there is a benevolent power superior to mine that can break seemingly unbreakable chains.

But for years, I couldn't see a *single* reason to be grateful for my attraction to men. That is no longer the case.

Despite (or, perhaps, partly due to) my attraction to men, the young me was a homophobe—seeing gays as less valuable than other people and, therefore, seeing myself as less legitimate than other people. Something astounding happened in my earliest nonsexual embraces a few years ago: One man I was holding had characteristics that were not attractive to me, but while holding him, I felt an overwhelming love, and I realized it was not my own love that I felt for him, but God's love for him.

Somehow, because I felt love for that gay man, I was able to feel love for myself, a man also attracted to men. I saw our value—his and mine—as rare beings. As soon as I loved me as I am, God's love for me burst through to my soul—as though I had been holding it at bay all my life. I always believed in my mind that God loved me, but I had imagined He couldn't love this *part* of me, so I hadn't allowed myself to *feel* His love until that moment. I don't believe God was ever withholding love; it's just that I couldn't feel what I hadn't accepted.

Today, I'm pleased with who I am *and* with my feelings. I know, not only in my mind but also in my heart, that God loves me. He has always seen my life with an attraction to men and has always lovingly had plans for this to become one of the best parts of my journey.

Not only does God love part of me and of you, He loves all of us *and* our differences. That doesn't mean He wants us to remain static or unchanging; I am saying He has a purpose for *all* the differences we compare ourselves to others with. He sees what differences can do toward granting us empathy and perfecting each other mutually.[3]

I believe in our eventual perfection, but this has never meant homogenization.[4] I won't debate whether God makes people gay—I only declare that He knows beforehand who will feel what and that the plan He makes with each of us includes using *any* of our differences to strengthen us and to bless us and others.

Today, thanks in part to ill health and family shortcomings (things I had viewed as devastating), I enjoy ongoing and deep connection, love, and acceptance with amazing people. I've learned I can love many people deeply without shortchanging others—and without possessiveness, guilt, or dependence.

I am grateful for my attraction to men. If offered a pill to become one hundred percent "straight," I doubt I would take it. I'm not saying that being heterosexual is less than, but knowing what I know about myself and the experiences I have with others because of my feelings, I believe I'm richer for the poignant separations, connections, and values I've gained because of attraction to those my own sex. Some of my experiences have been so profound, I doubt I could have had them under other circumstances. Difficulty and all, I would choose my own experience.

PATHS OF STARS

A big reason people are attracted to people is to experience deep and lasting connection (in a variety of forms and relationships). But look at any relationship around you; it seems there must be cosmic intervention to achieve relational peace, let alone bliss. I don't condemn anyone for disagreeing with my thoughts on same-sex relationship happiness at first glance. For some time, my own feelings and actions were quite against them! Thankfully, each of us can learn and grow!

An example of how we might embrace differences and difficulties for a higher purpose can be seen in my South

American mission experience. Even with my illness and the impact it has had on the rest of my life, if I had to choose between all I gained on my mission *or* having great health, without hesitation, I would keep my treasured missionary experiences and relationships. Even knowing beforehand how serving would affect my health, I would do it again in a heartbeat. My passport is still current.

YOUR UNIQUE PATH

Free will and natural consequence, light and dark, "good and evil," up and down are real paired principles or opposites—but not everything is binary, and *many* things fall outside of "right or wrong."[5] There are usually countless options, though seeing them may require contemplation.[6]

I believe that human relationships are eternal. I hope all people who feel attraction to their own sex—or who feel any potentially isolating difference—can learn its positive purpose and optimal expressions. I hope we find profound connections with others who feel "different" and gratitude for the enrichment that differences can bring. I hope you can perceive benefit in everything, and that you can escape any idea or situation that reduces choices.

The world needs you. I envision a non-distant day when pure same-sex affection is common—and no longer only an indicator of sexual relating. I see it happening now. If you don't see it, perhaps you're not looking for it. I often find what I look for. I've been in church with a man's arm around me—and we were warmly welcomed.

No one can be whole alone. I have presented some ways to meet needs and not necessarily burn relationship bridges. There are many gay couples that give up sex (or choose never to be sexual) and discover supernal connection that seems to only deepen.

The future of this planet is glorious. Your future is brilliant. You may have believed that your circumstance proved God was against you, but it could actually be evidence that He is working for your good. He has prepared paths for you to find lasting, loving relations now and always. I believe most everyone can find those paths with grace.[7] I've long been certain that heaven would be a place of love and affection with those dearest to me. Apparently, I'm already there.

NOTES

1. See William Shakespeare, *The Merchant of Venice* (New York: Gramercy Books, 1997), 223–224. Ultimately, no one will *demand* justice; it would mean a pound of flesh from each of us for harm we've caused, and none of us is without fault.

2. Knowledge is indeed power. See Bible, Luke 12:44, 13:28, 16:19–31; Rom. 8:17; Phil. 2:9; 2 Tim. 4:8; Rev. 3:21, 21:7.

3. Our differences make us *beautiful.* Anomalies like the Dead Sea or the Grand Canyon attract intense interest and wonder. The world would be very boring if everyone were the same.

4. "Christ's version of unity is about togetherness, not sameness." John K. Carmack, "Unity in Diversity," *Ensign*, March 1991, 7–9.

5. Take heart; *most* choices are a matter of individual taste and are not governed by law or commandment.
6. I still struggle with binary thinking!
7. For more information and resources on same-sex relating (regardless of orientation), overcoming old ways of thinking or compulsions, and increasing options, see: https://GayAdored.com.

Key Points

I'VE COVERED LOTS OF MATERIAL IN this book, and many ideas here may be new to you, or maybe they're old ideas from new angles. Whether you're queer or questioning yourself or you want to better understand a loved one, I hope this book is helpful to you. In that spirit, I've provided this list of key points to help you get a better grasp of what I've tried to share. Whether you've read the whole book or not, this summary of key points should be useful to you.

- I believe that relationships can be eternal and the source of our greatest joys. Yet, long-term relationship bliss (regardless of sexual orientation) requires help.
- Awareness of options increases power and satisfaction. By presenting multiple paths, I don't mean to imply that each is equally desirable—or that all are harmless.
- Sexual orientation is not contagious, a defect, a sin, a mortal choice, or an act of rebellion. We can exert influence over feelings, but often, we simply feel what we feel.

- God loves LGBTQIA persons! While this might not mean acceptance of gay sex as a positive expression of gayness, God has always known what we would feel and experience. His plan has always been that we could benefit from all of it.

- Free will/agency and opposition have always existed. While we have individual choice, we miss out/suffer when we ignore natural consequences.

- Few choices are binary. There are infinite ways to be human, let alone LGBTQIA. There may be better ways to love and be loved (regardless of orientation) than the standard ways the world signals.

- Human beings attracted to their own sex will likely remain so attracted for wonderful purposes. People of the same sex are designed to love each other powerfully—without possessiveness, guilt, or dependence—and *with no loss of love for anyone else* (love is limitless). While same-sex love isn't exclusive, it's possible that the person you have the deepest connection to—now and always—is the same sex as you.

- Like our need for oxygen, same-sex emotional needs are legitimate and ongoing. They must not be neglected.

- Emotional connection is a need. As good as it is, sexual euphoria is not love and doesn't satisfy true need. Confusing transitory euphoria for love can be a step toward falling out of "love" due to the fleeting nature of euphoria.

- Sex in itself isn't bad—but selfish/inappropriate sex, heterosexual or otherwise, disconnects us from the joy of union (and can be torture to escape; wanting more always leads to wanting more).

- While any sexual activity has the potential for selfishness, sexual stimulation between people of the same sex can result in emotional distancing—even for those who wait until they're in love—or, at minimum, distract participants from achieving the deepest emotional bonds. Few people have experienced the profound connection that can endure between people of the same sex who avoid being sexual with each other.

- Emotional needs can manifest as sexual desire, like feeling hungry when you're dehydrated. By neglecting true emotional connection, the feeling of neediness persists, regardless of how much sex one has. Meeting emotional needs healthfully can illuminate true needs, open previously unimagined relational possibilities, and might also reduce compulsive behavior.

- Celibacy and sobriety *don't* necessarily mean healthful or whole. A person can be sexual and sober, and a person can be celibate yet not sober.

- Authenticity is seeing self and others as divine. Most people prefer loving to being loved; giving love is deeply fulfilling.

- Hiding our differences and difficulties can lead to

destructive isolation. Honesty with trusted people can promote growth, bring liberating grace, and save us before a fall.

- The libido can be an indicator of how well or how poorly we are meeting emotional needs. You can work with your libido instead of battling it or being its slave. When emotional needs are met the libido becomes very calm; images and fantasy—even face-to-face propositions—lose their magnetism.

- Willpower—especially in human relations—cannot be our ultimate source of strength. There is power beyond our own.

- To relate with those of one's sex in a lasting fulfilling way, a person must gain their own conviction that:

  1. Your attraction to those of your sex is legitimate and exists for happiness.
  2. Non-sexual same-sex connection fulfills and creates lasting bonds.
  3. Same-sex sexual relations impede the deepest union.

- True connection and euphoria aren't mutually exclusive. Physical arousal is a normal biological reaction in human relating; it doesn't necessarily mean sex is on the agenda.

- Honest conversation is a super way to meet legitimate emotional needs—even without touch.

- Naked holding or indulging in same-sex sexual thoughts each distract from true connection.

- Same-sex bonds can be repaired/deepened. There are happy gay couples who are no longer (or never were) sexual, yet have been bonded for decades.
- Non-sexual same-sex connecting is not a technique to endure temptation—it satisfies legitimate needs, reduces frustration, and brings joyful relationships that can last forever.
- True intimacy can't be attained if one is out of sync with self or with the universe.
- Most choices, even mistakes, are not evil. Competing desires can help us learn who we are, what we value, what we are capable of. Individual worth doesn't change.
- The surest way to reduce options is to reject any constraint. Committing ourselves to principles/boundaries maximizes our freedom and choices. "Freeing" ourselves from boundaries and standards can enslave us to our own desires.
- Differences can bring us empathy and growth.
- A circumstance you believed to be negative might actually be to your benefit. Your most rewarding relationships may not be the one(s) you're currently in, pursuing, or think you're missing. They might result from the loss of relations or expectations previously held as important. Seeing abundant options might require modification to current notions.

Abundant Paths to Relating with a Gay Loved One—For Families of LGBTQIA Persons

(Please see LoveYourGayKid.com and chapters 2, 5, 6, 8, 9, 11, 12, and 13.)

"Go out into the darkness and put your hand into the Hand of God. That shall be to you better than light and safer than a known way." [1]

—*Minnie Louise Haskins*

YOU MAY JUST HAVE LEARNED THAT a loved one is LGBTQIA; your head may be swimming. It's normal to feel inadequate to even respond. One of the first feelings may be guilt—please don't hold on to that feeling.

May I offer you my assurance that regardless of what you or your loved one might feel at present, these differences—like all differences—are gifts that can bless us. When I finally figured out how these kinds of differences enrich my life, I was overwhelmed with how exquisite the gift of difference is. I would *never* alter what differences have brought me.

Like this book's title suggests, you don't have to choose between promoting unhealthful choices (which exist for everyone, regardless of orientation) and being hateful. There are far more loving and helpful responses.

WHEN LOVE ISN'T LOVE

Some of the worst pain in our lives can come from those closest to us—both via rejection and via too much "support" at the sacrifice of good judgment and even truth.[2] Some of us have heard of someone being disowned and/or kicked out of the house for being gay or of someone's partner being ignored or insulted by family.

You are *not* condoning sin by loving your LGBTQIA family member. Of course, you can still have expectations for behavior as long as they live in your home, just as you would for any family member. No family member should attack or demean your faith (and no one should demand that family choose between their faith and a family relationship). But you are *not* denying your faith by loving your LGBTQIA family member and their significant other; you are living it.

While the appendixes that follow offer specific supportive steps and resources for making healthful choices, here are some thoughts to expand your options and, hopefully, those of the people dear to you.

If the LGBTQIA individual is your child (or a child in your care), it's important to teach them resilience and to stand up for self, even with physical self-defense (hoping it won't be necessary). All bullying—psychosocial and physical—is to be taken seriously. If your child's bullies physically attack four or five at a time, as mine did, self-defense is moot. As soon as you're aware of a situation, *immediately* address it with teachers, youth leaders, administrators, law enforcement, and other authority figures who can help, and work with them toward resolution. Your child may not be the only victim. However, if the problem isn't handled immediately, get your child *out* of that environment, even if it is a "worship" environment!

Perhaps you cannot afford a more structured school or other environment; perhaps you don't have the luxury of home or private schooling (*truly* lamentable). If your child must remain in a public school or another less-structured environment, be persistent in exploring options for other classes, even other schools or districts. Do not back down until there is a place where bullying isn't tolerated.

If your child's school teaches human development or health courses (what was once called "sex ed"), advocate for age-appropriate curriculum that teaches inclusion but is balanced as to sexual expressions (hollow, isolating, unrestrained expressions must be countered by instruction on consequences and on expressions that foment lasting, boundary-respecting bonds that cherish all involved [see chapter 8]). Ideally, this guidance should come from *you*.[3]

Protect your child against those who (even in the name of love and support) too quickly or ill-advisedly encourage ideologies and choices that are harmful. Some individuals and families confuse divine confirmations of God's love (for them, for each person, for who we are right now) to be a divine endorsement of the world's hedonistic version of gay living. Some parents try so hard to support or not offend their children that they never challenge their child on any idea. Rather than be concerned for their child's *lasting* happiness, they try to put their child's comfort (or their own status with their child) above truth for fear that their child might not like them. Sacrificing truth in the name of love is neither helpful nor loving.

I believe God gave us differences so that we would learn from one another—and spread our love broadly. Of course, we sometimes bite our tongues (wisely) when someone isn't in a place to healthfully hear truth (and for better long-term relations). That situation is different from pretending that something harmful isn't harmful—or from outright encouraging the harmful things! To paraphrase myself, if a person hasn't experienced firsthand, long-term, sexually monogamous happiness in a same-sex union, perhaps they shouldn't encourage what they don't know is or isn't good for people.[4]

Unconditional love never equates to license—nor can it make consequences evaporate.[5] Unconditional love simply means that the object of our love can never do anything that would make us stop loving them, and this fact should be expressed!

I think the best thing one could do for an LGBTQIA child is to live our best life, modeling the advantages of self-discipline, grace, and love.

Additionally, protect your child against those who would paraphrase or spin discourse on gay topics as being hateful (unless preachers use epithets or condemn people rather than ideas). Be wary of "advocates" or "bridge builders" who demean or who think condescension is a good way to alter opposing positions.

Most parents want life to be fair for their kids. Yet, some parents accuse those who speak of non-sexual options of being haters. Why might some parents become incensed by added options for their child? This kind of sensitivity isn't advocacy. It facilitates self-deception and is misleading to kids and other impressionable people who are trying to identify who they are and what's important.

The devastating part of such sensitivity is that some well-meaning people could be contributing to someone's discouragement and despondency, even a child's. If someone discusses options for LGBTQIA people that include chastity, some parents (regardless of how the message is articulated) hear a bigot oppressing or condemning their child.[8] Some people paraphrase messages in such a light. Negative paraphrasing or message-spinning can cause LGBTQIA people to avoid hearing the *original* messages—meant to increase choices, were they heard directly from their authors. Does negative interpretation help a person avoid overwhelm and the feeling of rejection? I think it can foment it—perhaps more so than supportive statements by people earnestly encouraging contentment via mapping out positive choices.

I acknowledge that some leaders and laypeople have been (and even are today) bigoted and ignorant.[6] While change *is* needed in certain communities and in society at large, as charity director Sharon Eubank says, "I believe the change we seek in ourselves and in the groups we belong to will come less by activism and more by actively trying every day to understand one another."[7] What good does it do to interpret a path-multiplying message as being hurtful or hateful or to tell someone you love how they should feel or react? Telling another what to think is an effort to limit their choices. There are ways to support a loved one without hiding or whitewashing options. Help kids find peace with who they are and with where they are in their lives' journey: not shame, not pride, but *peace*.[8] If you hear a statement on LGBTQIA issues that rubs you the wrong way, perhaps the best thing to say to your LGBTQIA child is "I love you, and I'm sure that God does too."

With regard to gender identity, keep fluidity in mind. I believe that even intersex individuals (hermaphrodites) at some point attain a clear understanding of their eternal gender identity—despite initial doubts. I believe that in the eternities, *everyone* will be clear on their identity and will be ecstatic about it. Keep in mind, many people—including me—have experienced fluidity regarding physical attraction. Fluidity (even over decades) in gender identity is not uncommon.[9]

Encourage your child to be patient and thoughtful in self-discovery.[10] Even attractions unfold at different rates—and many early attractions aren't physical (see Appendix B). Yes, promise to keep your mind open, but wait until your child's brain is capable of adult reasoning before taking permanent steps, like agreeing to or facilitating surgery or a limiting philosophy or treatment that would be painful (or next to impossible) to undo. It is vital to evaluate *long-term* experiences and attitudes of many people who have experienced various options in this area.[11]

Awareness of mental health is critical:

Dr. Michelle Cretella, executive director of the American College of Pediatricians, told *The Christian Post* that [a] study "confirms what no one disputes: Namely, that youth who identify as LGBTQ have higher rates of mental illness leading to a greater risk of life-threatening behaviors." But contrary to what these authors conclude, Cretella said, there is "no evidence that 'destigmatizing efforts' will solve the problem, because there is no evidence that the higher rates are due primarily to stigmatization." She pointed out that Sweden is among the most LGBT affirming nations in the world, yet, LGBT mental illness and suicide rates in Sweden are just as dramatically elevated relative to the general population.[12]

"Improved mental health contributes to improved spirituality," says Steven J. Lund, "but research is showing the reverse is also true: improving spirituality improves mental health."[13]

I'm convinced that our choices help—or retard—our ability to grasp what brings lasting happiness; self-focused choices delay or interrupt our ability to even see the difference between a momentary comfort and enduring joy. In my experience, selfish choices impede my development (at minimum, they delay my happiness). Regardless, we must be patient with ourselves and others.

It is unhelpful to say that I or others will never want traditional marriage; no one but the individual can know that, (and then not always immediately). I'm contented now with my relationships and the possibilities—and choices—ahead.

FOR SPOUSES OF LGBTQIA PEOPLE

If you are married to someone attracted to their own sex, it can be overwhelming—even bewildering. But know this: Your opposite-sex spouse's sexual orientation has nothing at all to do with you. Neither is any addiction of theirs your responsibility. However, a spouse's attitudes about sex and intimacy—physical and emotional—may play a role in whether their partner seeks physical gratification outside the marriage. Bear in mind that the gender of a cheating spouse's other partner(s) is not a reflection of your fully realized masculinity or femininity.

My friend Tim is a bi man married to a heterosexual woman. After explaining to Tim's wife that he and I never get sexual (or naked) but that he and I share laughter, deep conversation, and affection, her concerns about Tim's needs and moral behavior have been greatly assuaged.

Isolation and ultimatums are unlikely to improve the situation. Just as no argument or threat of loss prevented me from acting on my addiction, no fear, heartbreak, pleading, or withdrawal on the part of a spouse will eliminate a person's legitimate social needs. While such expressions might *temporarily* alter behavior, we're not discussing being denied wants (like wanting a cookie), but legitimate needs. These are needs that don't go away—they must be met healthfully, in ongoing ways, or they become masters in undesirable ways (think Donner Party). Please see chapters 6, 8, and 9 on reducing risk via healthful same-sex relating. As we seek healthful ways to satisfy our needs for human connection, we can get past rational and irrational fears.

If one or both spouses have not kept their vows, counseling (individual and couple) is a helpful first step. I hope this book provides positive insight as to true needs and how to meet them. It is critical that both partners in a marriage understand such needs and meet them healthfully.

NOTES

1. Minnie Louise Haskins, "The Gate of the Year" (London: Hodder and Stoughton, 1940).

2.   Every human love, at its height, has a tendency to claim for itself a divine authority. Its voice tends to sound as if it were the will of God Himself. It tells us not to count the cost, it demands of us a total commitment, it attempts to override all other claims and insinuates that any action which is sincerely done "for love's sake" is thereby lawful and even meritorious. That erotic love and love of one's country may thus attempt to "become gods" is generally recognized. But *family* affection may do the same. So, in a different way, may friendship. Lewis, *The Four Loves*, 7, emphasis added.

3.   You may be concerned that your child might be indoctrinated into an LGBTQIA life. I have good and bad news: My experience is that—regardless of sexual experimentation or propaganda—a person eventually settles into what they know deep down reflects who they are (and their first guess is sometimes wrong; see Appendix B). Some people might be in their 30s or 50s before they really feel comfortable with who they are and what they are about! Experimentation, fluidity—even indoctrination—aren't uncommon, but don't let the notion that each person eventually figures self out make you neglectful, letting your child stumble unattended. Indoctrination might not affect them permanently, but premature sexual activity—and its frequent companions of sexual confusion and addiction—are topics far too complex and difficult for a child to deal with alone (apparently the brain is not fully developed until we're in our twenties). (FYI: Many kids who were molested by someone of their own sex never become gay, and many who weren't molested do.) Do everything you can to help them avoid these bumps. Parents: Six or seven years is *not* too early an age to begin

to discuss sex and personal boundaries with your child. Even younger children can grasp basic body safety and personal boundaries. And be completely aware of what others might be teaching your kids. See "At What Age Is the Brain Fully Developed?" Mental Health Daily, n.d., https://mentalhealthdaily.com/2015/02/18/at-what-age-is-the-brain-fully-developed/; The Alcohol Pharmacology Education Partnership, "Content: Brain Maturation Is Complete at about 24 Years of Age," Duke University, n.d., https://sites.duke.edu/apep/module-3-alcohol-cell-suicide-and-the-adolescent-brain/content-brain-maturation-is-complete-at-about-24-years-of-age/.

4. Some people behave as if love and truth are mutually exclusive—and loyalty should trump truth (because truth can sometimes be painful). Of course, we sometimes hold our tongues when someone isn't in a place to healthfully hear truth; yet, true loyalty doesn't withhold truth long-term, and it never misleads or lies. (Truth doesn't need us to shout or drone it incessantly.) Even if, for better long-term relations, we presently avoid certain topics, our pretending that something harmful isn't harmful—or encouraging something harmful—is neither love nor loyalty! Some people think loyalty is blind; they support poor choices because of *who* is making them. But devotion to truth is a better measure of loyalty: If someone truly loves you, they likely won't say that everything you do is good.

5. "We have to be careful that love and empathy do not get interpreted as condoning and advocacy, or that orthodoxy and loyalty to principle not be interpreted as unkindness or disloyalty to people." Jeffrey R. Holland, "The Cost—and

Blessings—of Discipleship," *Ensign*, May 2014, 8.

6. "Imperfect people are all God has ever had to work with. This must be terribly frustrating to Him, but He deals with it." Jeffrey R. Holland, "Lord, I Believe," *Ensign*, May 2013, https://www.churchofjesuschrist.org/study/general-conference/2013/04/lord-i-believe?lang=eng.

7. Sharon L. Eubank, "By Union of Feeling We Obtain Power with God," *Ensign*, November 2020, 55–57.

8. Rather than emulate shame—or pride—perhaps peace and hope should be our outlook. Some parents want to be dragon-like in defending their kids (the sentiment is understandable). Still, *pacific* might help us maintain an open mind—and have more influence with our children—long-term.

9. Please see chapters 5 and 6 on fluidity. While growing up, I had massive crushes on girls, though I was slow to experience physical attraction to them. See Gospel Topics, "Understanding Yourself," The Church of Jesus Christ of Latter-day Saints, https://www.churchofjesuschrist.org/topics/transgender/understanding?lang=eng

10. "There's nobody exactly like you. You're valuable." Sharon Eubank, "A Letter to a Single Sister."

11. See Ester di Giacomo et al., "Estimating the Risk of Attempted Suicide Among Sexual Minority Youths: A Systematic Review and Meta-analysis," *JAMA Pediatrics* 172, no. 12 (December 2018), 1145–52, https://doi.org/10.1001/jamapediatrics.2018.2731; Donald Antrim, "Finding a Way Back from Suicide," *The New Yorker*, August 9, 2021, https://www.newyorker.com/magazine/2021/08/16/finding-a-way-back-from-suicide; Susan Berry, "Science Says Transgender Hormones and Surgeries Do Not Prevent Suicides,"

Breitbart, June 30, 2021, https://www.breitbart.com/politics/2021/06/30/science-says-transgender-hormones-and-surgeries-do-not-prevent-suicides/; Kiley Crossland, "Sex Change Regret Silenced," *World*, October 6, 2017, https://world.wng.org/content/sex_change_regret_silenced; John Sexton, "One Woman's Story of Becoming a Trans Boy and Later Detransitioning," Hot Air (blog), February 21, 2022, https://hotair.com/john-s-2/2022/02/21/one-womans-story-of-becoming-a-trans-boy-and-later-detransitioning-n450114; Lizette Borreli, "Transgender Surgery: Regret Rates Highest in Male-to-Female Reassignment Operations," *Newsweek*, October 3, 2017, https://www.newsweek.com/transgender-women-transgender-men-sex-change-sex-reassignment-surgery-676777.

12. Leah MarieAnn Klett, "Gay, Transgender Youth at 'Significantly Higher Risk' of Suicide Than Heterosexual Peers: Study," *Christian Post*, December 18, 2018, https://www.christianpost.com/news/gay-transgender-youth-at-significantly-higher-risk-of-suicide-than-heterosexual-peers-study.html.

13. Steven J. Lund, "How the Children and Youth Program Strengthens Families," *Liahona*, March 2022, https://www.churchofjesuschrist.org/study/liahona/2022/03/united-states-and-canada-section/how-the-children-and-youth-program-strengthens-families?lang=eng. See also Sheldon Martin, "Strive to Be—A Pattern for Growth and Mental and Emotional Wellness," *Liahona*, August 2021, https://www.churchofjesuschrist.org/study/liahona/2021/08/strive-to-be-a-pattern-for-growth-and-mental-and-emotional-wellness?lang=eng; Erich

W. Kopischke, "Addressing Mental Health," *Liahona*, November 2021, 37–38; Reyna I. Aburto, "Thru Cloud and Sunshine, Lord, Abide with Me!" *Ensign*, October 2019, 58; Carolyn McNamara Barry et al., "Profiles of Religiousness, Spirituality, and Psychological Adjustment in Emerging Adults," *Journal of Adult Development* 27 (September 2020): 201–11, https://doi.org/10.1007/s10804-019-09334-z; Alen Malinovic et al., "Dimensions Of Religious/Spiritual Well-Being in Relation to Personality and Stress Coping: Initial Results from Bosnian Young Adults," *Journal of Spirituality in Mental Health* 18, no. 1 (2016): 43–54, https://doi.org /10.1080/19349637.2015.1059301; Shannon Gwin et al., "The Relationship between Parent–Young Adult Religious Concord and Depression," *Journal of Spirituality in Mental Health* 22, no. 1 (2020): 96–110, https://doi.org/10.1080/193 49637.2018.1549524.

Suggestions for Coming Out—If You Choose

D ON'T FEEL PRESSURE TO COME OUT. Ponder about when, how, and with whom to share your feelings. Follow good instincts. Consider whom you want to tell and why (whom you are attracted to is not necessarily everyone's business). If you don't want the whole world to know, the person or people you come out to must be trustworthy; you should have a good sense that they love you and are capable of keeping confidences. Therapists, counselors, and clergy are obligated to keep your personal information confidential unless they find you might hurt yourself or others (legally, they have a duty to report that).

Have a support system beyond those you plan to tell. This can be a therapist, clergy member, support group (most are anonymous), or other safe professional outside your family and friends.[1] There are LGBTQIA hotlines as well. (See the QR code at the end of the book.)

Consider outcomes. If you are financially dependent on your parents and there's a possibility that they might withdraw support or kick you out, it may be wise to wait until you have a backup plan for where to go and how to support yourself.

Neeral Sheth, a psychiatrist specializing in LGBTQIA health at Rush University, "advises against publicly coming out if you're just beginning. 'You might see celebrities coming out publicly through a social media post or a press conference, but I don't recommend doing anything like this—at least not until you have a core group of people that you know will support you 100%.' Social media can also be risky, as people you don't know well may make negative comments. And if even if you do know them, Sheth says that you should be prepared for people to have different reactions to your news, especially if they did not expect it."[2] Others, wanting to be supportive, may naively encourage you toward choices that may be destructive to you.

When it's the right time, a script may help you avoid misunderstandings. It may be good to prepare the person you're telling. Ask for what you need:

- "I'd like to speak with you tonight."
- "I want to tell you something; will you listen?"
- "Would you have time to talk? I have something I'd like to share with you; it may be difficult to hear."
- "I need you to keep this between us until I'm ready to share with others."

Speak what's in your heart. Here are some ideas:

- "You're important to me; I want you to know that I'm gay/bisexual/pansexual/lesbian/transgender/asexual/queer. This means that I (am attracted to ___/identify as ___)."
- "I've thought about this for a while and feel that . . ."
- "I'm not attracted to . . ."
- "This is hard for me" or "This is very personal."
- "It's been difficult hiding my true feelings."
- "I haven't mentioned this before because . . ."
- "I want to be honest with myself and with you because it's difficult to accept love or feel connection while wondering whether people would love or accept this part of me."
- "I'm sharing this because I love you and hope we can still have a good relationship."

Prepare for questions. Allow a loved one space and time to digest:

- "I'd like to talk more later, when you've had some time to think."
- "I'm happy to share what I can" or "I don't want to talk about details; I just wanted you to know."
- "I hope you will always accept me."
- "I'll try to answer your questions, but maybe not all at once."
- "I love you. Thank you for . . ."

If things don't go well, remember a person's *initial* response may not be what they intend. You may need to reassure them, set a boundary, or pause the conversation. Things may improve with time. Here are a few suggestions for how to handle a negative reaction:

- "I know you're concerned/angry; I still love you."
- "I'm still the same person you've always known."
- "I don't want to fight; I hope you'll change your mind."
- "I'm going to take a break, but I will be back at . . ."
- "I need to stop for now; perhaps we can talk later."[3]

NOTES

1. Support for LGBTQIA people: LoveYourGayKid.com, https://www.northstarlds.org/; suicide hotline: 988 (1-800-273-8255); https://www.focusonthefamily.com/get-help/counseling-services-and-referrals/.

2. MK Manoylov and Zil Goldstein, "How to Come Out to Your Friends, Family Members, and More—And How to Make Sure It's Healthy and Safe for You," Insider, January 20, 2021, https://tinyurl.com/ycka492y.

3. See "Coming Out to Your Parents," Strong Family Alliance, 2017, https://www.strongfamilyalliance.org/how-to-come-out-to-parents/.

4. Information enhanced with ideas from ChurchofJesusChrist.org, Asha French, Caitlin Ryan, Family Acceptance Project, and Bianca Salvetti, "How to Talk to Your Child Who Is Questioning or Identifies as

Lesbian, Gay, Bisexual, Transgender, Queer or Asexual (LGBTQIA)," RN Remedies (blog), Children's Hospital Los Angeles, June 24, 2016, https://www.chla.org/blog/rn-remedies/how-talk-your-child-who-questioning-or-identifies-lesbian-gay-bisexual-transgender.

How to Respond When a Loved One Comes Out to You (& What Not to Do)

IN ADDITION TO THIS SECTION, YOU may find it helpful to review the list of Key Points as well as chapters 2, 5, 6, 8, 9, 10, and 11.

Coming out may be a time of complex emotions and reactions for all involved, but a simple expression of love has the power to calm and reassure. If you don't know what to say, you can always say, "I love you." You don't have to understand your loved one's situation to express your love for them.

While it is typically unproductive to tell a child they are

simply going through a phase when they come out to you, discovering identity *is* a process—and what one thought was set in stone can evolve. It has for me and others.

My friend Jay came out to his parents as gay when he was a young adult. He laughs because, contrary to what he predicted, his stern dad—not his sweet mom—took the news in stride (his mom had to go compose herself in the other room). What *none* of them anticipated was that a while later, Jay realized that he didn't want a gay partnership (at least not in the common definition); he discovered he is asexual! "Questioning" is a real state.

Patience with self, loved ones, and God is always a good thing. Here are some other ideas to help you and your loved ones:

- Listen. Ask questions.
- Thank them for telling you. Assure them, "I will always love you."
- Believe that your loved one can have a happy life as an LGBTQIA person (and that gender and sexual orientation are only a part of a much broader identity and life).
- If you need time to digest the news, assure your loved one that you love them and ask for some time to take it in. Follow up—and don't delay this! Check in every once in a while.
- If you learn about your loved one's same-sex attraction secondhand, don't take it personally.
- If you react poorly, apologize.

- Where comfortable for both, give affection. Be courageous. Some teens give a vibe that they don't want hugs, but they often really do.

- Stand up for your loved one if anyone (including family) is disrespectful. You don't have to advocate a certain lifestyle—but every person deserves love and respect.

- Research different perspectives and data—don't rely on your loved one to be your only source of information.

- If your loved one is living with you, don't alter your standards for them. Be sure they understand your expectations, and encourage wise and healthful choices. If the person is a minor, regular conversations about sexual responsibility are essential—regardless of orientation (see chapters 5–7 and 9–13). These conversations don't have to be formal but can be in the course of other activities.[1]

- Always get permission before sharing about your loved one with someone else.

- Where appropriate, humbly share your experiences and challenges with others.

- Welcome your loved one's partner or LGBTQIA friends to your home and to family gatherings. This is not a surrender of your personal moral standards; it is loving one's neighbor (and, hopefully, retaining positive influence with your loved one).

- If your loved one expresses any suicidal thoughts or desires, or a desire to harm themselves, get them professional help.[2]
- Try to honor a transgender (or any) person's wishes regarding name choice. It shouldn't be difficult to use whatever name a person chooses. If you cannot bring yourself to call your trans loved one their preferred pronoun, ask if they'd be okay with you using terms like *you/they/their*. Be patient with each other, as it takes time to replace old habits with new ones.
- Continue to love and serve your loved one. The least productive question to ask (yourself or anyone) is "Why?" It's also unproductive to ask God or others to "fix/heal/change" your loved one. Helpful questions include the following: "How can I help? How can I be the support my loved one needs? How can we learn from this?"
- Encourage loved ones to confide in honest people. A person's devotion to truth, not just love, is an excellent measure of potential loyalty and sound counsel.

QUESTIONS YOU MIGHT ASK

- "What does gay (or bi, etc.) mean for you?"
- "What has it been like discovering this?"
- "How are you feeling now?"
- "How can I best support you?"

THINGS TO AVOID

- Don't bemoan a "sad" situation (verbally or otherwise), and don't ignore or pretend like you didn't hear the information. Don't name-call or criticize gays or queers in general.
- Don't feel guilty. If the loved one is your offspring, remember that while you may not have been a perfect parent, your parenting likely has nothing to do with your child's sexual orientation or gender identity.
- Don't assign stereotypes to your loved one (e.g., that they likely have great fashion sense, have mechanical or sports ability, or should be a natural dancer).
- Don't exclude your LGBTQIA loved one from activities or family gatherings. (Don't worry what other people might think of you!) Don't pressure your loved one to tell/not tell certain people.
- Don't insult, ignore, yell, hit, or physically hurt your loved one or pressure them to be more (or less) masculine or feminine. Don't restrict your loved one's access to *rational* friends, resources, activities, or organizations for fear they'll choose "gay life."

AVOID SAYING

- "Don't you think you should try dating the opposite sex?"

- "Are you sure?" (Though, keep my friend Jay in mind!)
- "I knew it all along." (Maybe you did, but so what?)
- "Don't you know what the scriptures say about this? God doesn't want gays. He punishes them." (This is inaccurate and harmful.)
- "This is probably just a phase." (That's possible, but when earlier pains or changes arose for your loved one, did you ignore those?)
- "Please don't tell anyone else." That's your insecurity talking; this is about your loved one, not you.
- "I hope you won't be flamboyant about this." (You allow others free expression; allow your loved one to determine how they express themselves.)

CONSIDER

- Does this knowledge change the deep emotions you felt when this person entered your life or the feelings you've had for this person to this point?
- You will never regret showing love or saying "I love you" to a loved one. You will never regret listening and trying to understand.
- It's natural to grieve. Do you feel your dream of the "perfect" family slipping away? Do you fear losing a close relationship? Are you afraid your loved one won't be treated with kindness? These feelings are natural. There is no shame in grieving.
- Blaming yourself or others is neither warranted nor helpful.

(See: LoveYourGayKid.com. Information enhanced with ideas from ChurchofJesusChrist.org, Asha French, Caitlin Ryan, Family Acceptance Project, and Salvetti, "How to Talk to Your Child.")

How to Support Parents & Families of LGBTQIA People

DON'T BE SILENT OR PULL AWAY; don't ignore; don't speculate regarding the family member's choices—what they are doing or not doing—alone or with others. See chapters 1, 2, and 5 before making any comments about causation or choice or change. Don't worry what your association with LGBTQIA people might imply to others; model fearless love!

Try not to make assumptions about anyone's sexual orientation or gender. Don't lecture or simplify or brush LGBTQIA issues aside. Don't make assumptions about the family member's future. Don't raise eyebrows when LGBTQIA people are given jobs in church.

Visit. Offer empathy, love, and support. Reach out to the family member, too. Give hugs. Tell them you love them.

Educate yourself on related topics. Ask sincere questions in an effort to understand and then listen. Try to imagine how these families might feel.

ASK

- "How is _____ ?" (If the loved one is a child, ask about *all* their children.)
- "How can I help you and your family member know you're all loved?"
- "Is there something that might help your loved one feel more welcome at church/school/etc.?"

SAY

- "I love your family member and your family; we want to be friends with you!"
- "We need LGBTQIA people around us. Each is important and valuable!"
- "I love and accept your family member just as they are!"
- "I may not know what it is like to be in your shoes as the parents/family of a gay individual, but I would really like to understand."
- "I never want to say the wrong thing or anything hurtful, so please tell me if I do."
- "Your family member is welcome in my home."
- "I won't try to give unsolicited advice, but I'm always here if you need to talk."
- "No judgment here!"

- "I want your family member to be healthy and happy. I will try to support in healthful ways."

See: LoveYourGayKid.com. Information enhanced with ideas from ChurchofJesusChrist.org, Asha French, Caitlin Ryan, Family Acceptance Project, and Salvetti, "How to Talk to Your Child." For more information and resources on same-sex relating (regardless of orientation), overcoming old ways of thinking or compulsions, and increasing options, see: https://GayAdored.com (QR code below).

To the Reader

I HOPE YOU FOUND THIS BOOK TO be helpful. Get a free relationships checklist when you pre-order my 2025 workbook, *The Joys of Male Connection: Abundant Paths to Solid, Rewarding, Lasting Relationships*. It includes: worksheets, exercises/activities, quizzes, blueprints, next steps, tips, insightful quotes, fill-in-the-blank exploration, and a progress tracker—all to help you to walk well with others. Don't miss these concise concepts and tools.

Do you have a deep sense of lack in your life, something that nothing seems to satisfy? I've talked at length about social and emotional needs, but we have other needs as well. It may be a space that nothing on earth can fill; it may be a deep longing for God. While social needs must be met by other human beings, your God need is also real. Just as God will not fill our human needs, humans cannot fill our God need. Regular worship in temple, church, mosque, or synagogue can help fill this need. While a person can call upon God and read His words anywhere, doing so with others has significant impact on our faith and hope.

A more spiritual version of this book is called, *God Adores You: Beyond Either/Or Thinking to Your Most Fulfilling Relationships*.

Get Bonus Material (QR code last page)!

RECOMMENDED READING

C. S. Lewis, *The Four Loves* (Boston, New York: Mariner Books, 2012)

Chip Heath and Dan Heath, *Decisive: How to Make Better Choices in Life and Work* (New York: Crown Business, 2013)

Gary Chapman, *The 5 Love Languages: The Secret to Love that Lasts* (Winston-Salem: Northfield Publishing, 2014)

Sexaholics Anonymous (Brentwood, TN: Sexaholics Anonymous, 1984)

Meghan Decker, *Tender Leaves of Hope: Finding Belonging as LGBTQ Latter-day Saint Women* (Springville, UT: Cedar Fort, 2022)

Karl Beckstrand, *God Adores You* (Midvale, UT: Paths Press, September 2022)

Karl Beckstrand, *Men Need Men: Building Lasting Satisfying Relationships—Regardless of Sexual Orientation* (workbook. Midvale, UT: Paths Press, 2025)

Karl Beckstrand, *Women Need Women: Building Lasting Satisfying Relationships—Regardless of Sexual Orientation* (workbook. Midvale, UT: Paths Press, 2025)

If you like, please rate this book online—and, of course, share these titles with other readers!

OTHER POPULAR TITLES by Karl Beckstrand:

The Joys of Male Connection: Abundant Paths to Solid, Rewarding, Lasting Relationships (secular workbook. 2025)

The Bridge of the Golden Wood: A Parable on How to Earn a Living

No Offense: Communication Guaranteed Not to Offend

To Swallow the Earth: A Western Thriller

Horse & Dog Adventures in Early California: Short Stories & Poems (with Ransom Wilcox)

Bright Star, Night Star: An Astronomy Story

GROW: How We Get Food from Our Garden

Agnes's Rescue

Anna's Prayer

Ida's Witness: The True Story of an Immigrant Girl

Samuel Sailing: The True Story of an Immigrant Boy

Crumbs on the Stairs – Migas en las escaleras: A Mystery

4 Spanish-English Books for Kids

Gopher Golf: A Wordless Picture Book

Bad Bananas: A Story Cookbook

She Doesn't Want the Worms

Muffy & Valor: A True Dog Story

PremioPublishing.com

BONUS MATERIAL

GAYADORED.COM OR QR CODE

www.ingramcontent.com/pod-product-compliance
Lightning Source LLC
Chambersburg PA
CBHW031509270326
41930CB00006B/323